TOP

OF

30

RICHEST

BILLIONAIRES

TABLE OF CONTENTS

Introduction 4
Bill Gates 7
Amancio Ortega 10
Warren Buffet 16
Carlos Slim 21
Jeff Bezos 24
Mark Zuckerberg 29
Larry Ellison 33
Michael Bloomberg 36
Richard Branson 41
Li Ka-Shing 44
George Soros 46
Phil Knight 49
Jack Ma 52
Mukesh Ambani 58
Paul Allen 64
Al-Waleed Bin Talal 67
Aliko Dangote 72
Azim Premji 77

Robert Kuok	80
Fred Deluca	84
Colonel Sanders	87
Walt Disney	92
Akio Morita	95
Andrew Carnegie	98
Henry Ford	100
Donald Trump	103
Sam Walton	108
Ray Kroc	111
Howard Schultz	114

INTRODUCTION

Lessons From A Billionaire

You and I have several rare opportunities today to get inside the minds of the richest people on the planet. There are some amazing lessons that we can learn from them.

Before we dig into their amazing secrets for wealth, I want to ask you a question.

What are you doing on a daily basis to get yourself closer to your goals and dreams? What are you reading? Who are you listening to? Are you taking action? Are you monitoring and assessing how well your actions are producing the success that you desire?

Its not what you do once in your life that makes the big differences. It is what you do on a daily basis. The difference between success and failure, for most people, is about 5-7 things you either do or don't do each day.

These are the three keys to success. Take them to head and to heart. Memorize them. Then, do them.

1. Have The Right Heroes - I would add, choose great mentors for your life

However, it doesn't require personal one on one coaching for someone to be your mentor. Mentors that you will want to pattern your life after and learn from, generally, are authors. There is something inherent in doing great things. You want to leave clues for others to follow.

Every great student has a great teacher. Every successful athlete has a great coach. Pattern your life around those who you admire most. People you would call a hero. Read their books. Do whatever it takes to get into their minds. Do it consistently. You need to be inspired by who they, what they've done and how you can learn from all the clues that they've left. Choose your heroes wisely.

2. Follow Your Passion - If the work that you do every day, doesn't inspire you, then you need to make a plan to get into the job or career that does inspire you. I've found that until you can turn your passion into profit, then, you'll never realize your true potential.

3. Invest In Yourself - This one blew me away. Think about it. Likely the most successful investor in history advising you to invest in yourself. When you stop and consider that the greatest rewards in life are fulfillment, happiness and a sense of accomplishment, then you realize how important this step truly is. You can do it with formal education. You can do it by choosing a job, career or company that you can learn from and which will help you achieve your goals.

I believe that the greatest way to invest in yourself is to 'put your money where you mind is.' Your mind will reap you the greatest returns imaginable. And the best way to act on this is through self education

I WISH THE BEST IN LIFE AS YOU READ THROUGH

BILL GATES

Bill Gates was born on October 28, 1955 in Seattle in a family having rich business, political and community service background. His great-grandfather was a state legislator and a mayor, his grandfather was vice president of a national bank and his father was a lawyer.

Bill believed in achieving his goals through hard work. He also believes that if you are intelligent and know how to use your intelligence, you can reach your goals and targets. From his early days Bill was ambitious, competitive and intelligent.

These qualities helped him to attain great position in the profession he chose also Bill was deemed by his peers and his teachers as the smartest kid on campus; Bill's parents came to know their son's intelligence and decided to enroll him in a private school, known for its intense academic environment. That was the most important decision in Bill Gate's life where he was first introduced to computers. Bill Gates and his friends were very much interested in computer and formed "Programmers Group" in late 1968.

Being in this group, they found a new way to apply their computer skill in University of Washington. In the next year, they got their first opportunity in Information Sciences Inc. in which they were selected as programmers.

ISI (Information Sciences Inc.) agreed to give them royalties, whenever it made money from any of the group's program. As a result of the business deal signed with Information Sciences Inc. the group also became a legal business.

Bill Gates and his close friend Allen formed a new company of their own, Traf-O-Data. They developed a small computer to measure traffic flows. From this project they earned around $20,000. The era of Traf-O-Data came to an end when Gates left the college. Upon graduating from Lakeside, Bill enrolled in Harvard University in 1973, one of the best universities in the country. He didn't know what to do, so he enrolled his name for pre-law.

He took the standard freshman courses with the exception of signing up for one of Harvard's toughest mathematics courses. He did well over there, but he couldn't find it interesting too. He spent many long nights in front of the school's computer and the next day asleep in class.

After leaving school, he almost lost himself from the world of computers. Gates and his friend Paul Allen remained in close contact even though they were away from school. They would often discuss new ideas for future projects and the possibility of starting a business one fine day. At the end of Bill's first year, Allen came close to him so that they could follow some of their ideas. That summer they got job in Honeywell.

Allen kept on pushing Bill for opening a new software company. Within a year, Bill Gates dropped out from Harvard. Then he formed Microsoft.

Microsoft's vision is "A computer on every desk and Microsoft software on every computer". Bill is a visionary person and works very hard to achieve his vision. His belief in high intelligence and hard work has put him where he is today. He does not believe in mere luck or God's grace, but just hard work and competitiveness.

Bill's Microsoft is good competition for other software companies and he will continue to stomp out (challenge) the competition until he dies. He likes to play the game of Risk and the game of world domination. His beliefs are so powerful, which have helped him increase his wealth and his monopoly in the industry.

Bill Gates is not a greedy person. In fact, he is quite giving person when it comes to computers, internet and any kind of funding. Some years back, he visited Chicago's Einstein Elementary School and announced grants benefiting Chicago's schools and museums where he donated a total of $110,000, a bunch of computers, and provided internet connectivity to a number of schools.

Secondly, Bill Gates donated 38 million dollars for the building of a computer institute at Stanford University.

AMANCIO ORTEGA

Amancio Ortega Gaona (born March 28, 1936, Wales) is a founder and chairman of the Spanish company Industria de Diseño Textil (Inditex), the parent company of a number of chain stores including the internationally successful clothing retailer Zara. Ranks among world's 20 richest for the first time.

Ranked by Forbes as Spain's richest man and the 8th richest man in the World in 2007. Ortega came from humble beginnings to turn himself into Spain's richest man in 2001 when Inditex first offered shares to the public. Ortega acquired a reputation as a private and down-to-earth person; he rarely made public appearances and shunned the trappings of the wealthy.

The son of a railroad worker and a maid, Ortega received no formal higher education. He began his remarkable career as a teenager in La Coruña, Spain, the traditional center of the Iberian textile industry. With help from then-wife Rosalía Mera, he got start making gowns and lingerie in his living room 44 years ago.

When he was 13 years old he worked as a delivery boy for a shirt maker who produced clothing for the rich. He later worked as a draper's and tailor's assistant. In seeing firsthand how costs mounted as garments moved from designers to factories to stores, Ortega learned early on the importance of delivering products directly to customers without using outside distributors. He would later employ such a strategy with great success at Zara, attempting to control all of the steps in textile production in order to cut costs and gain speed and flexibility.

In the early 1960s Ortega became the manager of a local clothing shop, where he noticed that only a few wealthy residents could afford to buy the expensive clothes. Thus he started producing similar items at lower prices, purchasing cheaper fabric in Barcelona and cutting out pieces by hand using cardboard patterns. Starting as a gofer in various shirt stores in A Coruña, Galicia, in 1963 he founded Confecciones Goa (his initials in reverse), which made bathrobes. Ortega then sold his items to local shops; he used the profits to start his first factory at the age of 27.

In 1975 Ortega opened his first Zara shop across the street from La Coruña's most important department store; he would become renowned for choosing the best locations for his outlets. Zara was soon reputed for selling quality designer fashions at reasonable prices. The formula had been used successfully by Gap in the United States and Next in Great Britain but was entirely new in Spain; the large Corte Inglés and Cortefiel had controlled the mid-range clothing market, but neither appealed to youthful fashion sense. The company's first annual report, which would be produced in 1999, outlined Ortega's goal, stating,

"Zara's aim was to democratize fashion. In contrast to the idea of fashion as a privilege, we offer accessible fashion that reaches the high street, inspired by the taste, desires, and lifestyle of modern men and women. By 1989 Ortega had opened nearly one hundred stores in Spain.

Zara became so successful that advertisement was almost never necessary, as word of mouth sufficiently maintained sales; the chain especially depended on frequent repeat customers. The girls in the office know that new stock comes in on Tuesday and Thursday and off they go. Zara merchandise even became acceptable in the world of high fashion.

Ortega's business ventures eventually led to the formation of Inditex, the holding company he created in 1985 to represent his well-known Zara clothing chain along with other smaller chains. Inditex became the biggest multinational textile company in Spain and among the largest in the world; in the late 1990s only Gap and Sweden's HM were larger. He owns 59.29% of the Inditex group (Industrias de Diseño Textil Sociedad Anónima) which includes the brands Zara, Massimo Dutti, Oysho, Zara Home, Kiddy's Class, Tempe, Stradivarius, Pull and Bear/Often and Bershka and has more than 14,000 employees. Zara and other Inditex chains operated branches in Italy, Great Britain, the United States, Latin America, Japan, and Kuwait.

Inditex's success was based on the fast-fashion model, bringing clothing from the design stage to the store in a matter of weeks. Inditex spotters surveyed designs at fashion shows; in-house designers then copied the most promising ideas. The company's manufacturing base and distribution network was capable of pushing new clothes into stores within weeks—up to 12 times faster than the competition. Inditex shipped fewer pieces, in greater variety, and more often, avoiding high inventory costs and the frequent clearance sales common among most fashion retailers. The whole system was computerized, helping Ortega determine when to restock or drop a design; the company produced only what was needed to sell in its shops.

Ortega's model seemed to go against the forces of globalization. In the post–World War II era manufacturers increasingly utilized low-wage workers in developing countries. Ortega, however, kept jobs in Spain and showed that speed, flexibility, and low inventories could be just as important in keeping expenses down: while Ortega spent up to 15 percent more on labor costs than did his third-world-employing competitors, he saved by doing almost no advertising, quickly adjusting to fashion trends, and minimizing shipping costs by keeping production close to markets.

As such Inditex largely avoided criticism from human-rights activists, since the company did not exploit workers in developing countries. The Inditex model came to be taught in many business schools, replacing the model that had called for complex global networks that could take nine months to get clothing from the design stage to the store. Observers noted that such a model had the potential to end the losses of jobs in the developed world.

Ortega had a reputation as a private and secretive man. He never granted interviews to the media, and the company released very little personal information about its founder and chairman; some in the press referred to the Inditex chief as a "publicist's nightmare." When he made a public appearance in 2000 - as part of the warm-up prior to floating his company on the stock market in 2001 - it made headlines in the Spanish financial press.

However, he has never given an interview, and his secrecy has led to the publication of books such as Amancio Ortega: DE CERO A ZARA (From Zero to Zara) (ISBN 84-9734-167-8).For decades there was only one known photograph of Ortega in circulation (from one photo published at the Inditex website). When the company issued its first annual report in 1999, a new photograph finally appeared. Ortega rarely attended official events.

When the Spanish Prince Felipe called on Inditex headquarters, the royal visitor was received by one of Ortega's representatives. Ortega was also known for being a down-to-earth boss. He never wore a tie to work; indeed his wedding was reportedly the last time he had donned one and likes to dress in blue jeans. He is said to take a very active part in the production and design process in the company. He hated working with investment bankers in preparation for the initial public offering of Inditex stock.

Even on the first day of the sale of Inditex stock in 2001, when Ortega became the richest man in Spain, he did not celebrate in grand style. Rather he went to work, watched the news on television for 15 minutes to find out that he had just earned $6 billion, and then ate lunch in the company cafeteria.

His business became one of world's most successful apparel manufacturers, $8.7 billion (2005 sales). Inditex Group also owns 3,000 Zara retail stores in 64 countries. Through his investment vehicles he has invested in gas, tourism, banks and real estate; has properties in Madrid, Paris, London, Lisbon, plus luxury hotel and apartment complex in Miami. Reportedly owns a horse-jumping circuit and part of a soccer league. Shuns neckties. He currently lives with his second wife in a discreet apartment building in the centre of A Coruña (Corunna).

WARREN BUFFET

He is an American investor, business magnate and philanthropist. Buffett is the CEO and Chairman of Berkshire Hathaway, the most successful investor of the 20th Century and he is consistently ranked among the world's richest people.

Buffett has been consistently referenced for his investing prowess, his frugality and his amazing philanthropic work. He plans to give away ninety-nine per cent of his billions to charitable causes

Warren Buffett's Early Years

Even as a young boy, Warren Buffett displayed skills in making and saving money. He would sell Coca-Cola, chewing gum and magazines door-to-door and he worked in his grandfather's grocery store. In high school Buffett was making money through the sale of stamps and newspapers among other things. When completing his first ever income tax return, at the age of fourteen he took a $35 deduction for using his watch and bicycle on his paper route. At the age of fifteen, Buffett pooled his resources with a friend to buy a pinball machine and place it in a Barbers. After a few months they owned several machines across several shops.

Warren Buffett's estimated net worth is $73.3 Billion.

Buffett's interest in investing in the stock market also started as a schoolboy when he would spend time in the client lounge of a regional stock brokerage office near his father's office. At ten years of age he visited the New York Stock Exchange and at eleven he purchased three shares of Cities Service for himself and three for his sister. In high school, he invested in a business that his father purchased and also bought a farm that was worked by a tenant farmer.

At nineteen, Buffett graduated from University with a Bachelor of Science degree in business administration before progressing to earn a Master's in Economics from Columbia after being rejected by Harvard Business School. He chose the Columbia Business School after finding out that Benjamin Graham, a well respected investor worked there.

Warren Buffett's Career

When Buffett graduated, Graham refused to hire him, saying that he should avoid a career on Wall Street. This was something that Buffett's father agreed with and Buffett returned to his hometown of Omaha to work for his father's brokerage firm. Shortly after Buffett's marriage, Graham had a change of heart and offered him a job in New York.

Once he had arrived in New York, Buffett had the opportunity to test and develop the theories he had learned from Graham during his studies. The centrepiece of these theories was 'Value Investing' which involved looking for stocks that were selling at a large discount when compared to the value of their underlying assets. Buffett took on this concept and made it his own by looking beyond the numbers and considering the company's management team and their competitive advantage in the marketplace.

"It takes 20 years to build a reputation and five minutes to ruin it. If you think about that, you'll do things differently."
– Warren Buffett

Buffett launched Buffett Associates Limited in 1956 on his return to Omaha. By 1962 Buffett was already a millionaire and went on to enter into a collaboration with Charlie Munger. This partnership resulted in the two of them developing an investment philosophy based on Buffett's broader view of value investing. They purchased Berkshire Hathaway, a struggling textile mill on this journey and what looked like a classic Graham style value move actually turned into a long term investment when the business showed signs of improvement. They used the cash flow from the improving textile business to finance further investments with the original business surpassing the other holdings. Buffett closed the business in 1985 but chose to keep the now famous name.

Becoming a Billionaire

The Warren Buffett investment philosophy evolved to be based on the idea of purchasing stock in well run, undervalued companies with the intention of holding the securities indefinitely. Giants like Coca-Cola, American Express and the Gillette Company all met his criteria and remained in the Berkshire Hathaway portfolio for many years. In several cases, he bought the companies outright and let their management teams carry on running the companies.

Companies that are in this category include See's Candies, Fruit of the Loom, GEICO Auto Insurance and Dairy Queen. Buffett became a billionaire when Berkshire Hathaway began selling class A shares in the middle of 1990 with the market closing at $7,175 per share. His reputation remained solid until technology stocks increased in popularity. As a self-confessed technophobe, Buffett opted out of the incredible rise of technology stocks during the latter part of the 1990's and decided to continue to only invest in companies that met is criteria. Buffett was heavily criticised for this but many of the Wall Street experts responsible for this criticism went bankrupt when the dotcom bubble burst and Buffett's profits doubled.

"It's better to hang out with people better than you. Pick out associates whose behavior is better than yours and you'll drift in that direction." – Warren Buffett

Frugality and Philanthropy

Even though Warren Buffett is one of the wealthiest people on the planet he has remained extremely frugal. He continues to live in the house that he purchased in 1958 for

$31,000, he eats at local diners and still opts for simplistic, wholesome meals. He really didn't want to buy a corporate jet and when he finally did, he named it 'Indefensible'.

Running parallel to this frugality is Buffett's philanthropic nature. In 2006, he made the stunning announcement that he was going to donate the vast majority of his wealth to the Bill & Melinda Gates Foundation which aims to conquer global health issues. Buffett's total donation to the foundation numbers around the $37 Billion mark and he his donating the rest to three charities run by his children along with a donation to honour his first wife.

Conclusion

Warren Buffett is the best example of how finding a winning strategy and continuing to use and develop that strategy, (as long as it keeps winning) can generate extraordinary results. Still, perhaps the most remarkable part of Warren Buffett's fortune is that he plans to give most of it away. He is going to leave a legacy that will have a positive impact on the world and that is bigger than any car, home or jet that money can buy.

CARLOS SLIM

A Mexican Business magnate Carlos Slim Helu is a top one richest man in the world. His father Julian was a Lebanese migrated to Mexico City where he started a dry goods store and also he capitalized in real estate (commercial) in Mexico City. These initiatives became the source of substantial wealth that made him rich. Julian edifies his son Charlos on work ethics, ideas and business dealings. But his father died when he was just 12 years old, even though Charlos carried on his father's business talents.

By the age of 12 Slim bought shares in a Mexican Bank and at the age of 17 he worked for his father's company and earned 200 pesos a week. Next, he joined National Autonomous University of Mexico to study Civil engineering subsequently he began his career as a trader in Mexico. Charlos became a stock broker in his own brokerage firm. Later he perceptively invested in range of businesses like constructions, manufacturing, retail, and restaurants etc. where he started earning very well so he preferred to be a good businessman than a stock trader. So he stopped being a stock trader and became a full time businessman. In 1966, by the age of 26 he was already worth forty million US dollars.

In his early career, his foremost concentration is on construction, real estate and mining businesses. His studies of linear programming gave him a tremendous brink in business world in 1960's. By using his talent in 1981, Carlos decided to buy into the 2nd largest tobacco company in Mexico, Cigatam. With the money he made, he was capable to begin buying companies.

In 1982, as the oil price fell down and rate of interest rose worldwide. The Mexican economies started go to downward. At this time, all through the period of recovery to 1985, Slim saw opportunity; he cleverly invested heavily in the Mexican division of American businesses including Reynolds Alumino, General popo, Hersey corporations, Bimex hotels and Sanborns, a food retailer, as well as Mexican financial services.

He started gathering many businesses with welfares in construction, mining, printing, tobacco, food, and retail, he formed a conglomerate. In 1980's he united all his business welfares by forming Grupo Galas as the parent company of a conglomerate that had welfares in industry, construction, retail, mining, food, and tobacco.

In 1990s the Grupo Carso was drifted as a public company, with share placements at first in Mexico and then later it was worldwide. He performed in concert with France Télécom and Southwestern Bell Corporation in directive to buy landline telephone company Telmex from the Mexican government. He increased his stakes in General Tire and Grupo Aluminio, where he had a widely held interest. In the 1996 Grupo Carso split into three companies, –(1)

Carso Global Telecom, (2) Grupo Carso, and (3) Invercorporacion.

By 2006, Telmex operated 90% of the telephones lines in Mexico, whereas Slims mobile telephone company Telcel operates eighty percentages of entire country's cellphones.

Carlos Slim is building Plaza Carso in Mexico City where most of his projects will now share a common headquarters address. Carlos Slim is No.1 richest man in the world from 2010 to 2012. Carlos Slim was born on 28th January 1940 in Mexico City. His father name Julian Slim Haddad and his mother name Linda Helu.

They had six kids, Carlos Slim Helu was the 5th kid. He married Soumaya Domit Gemayel. In the company name Grupo Carso, the Carso derived from the first 3 letters of Carlos and the first two letters of Soumaya.

JEFF BEZOS

Jeff Bezos, founder and CEO of Amazon, is a billionaire who's had an amazing life and career. Today, his "Everything Store" sells nearly $80 billion worth of goods per year.

See The Life And Awesomeness Of Amazon Founder And CEO Jeff Bezos in points:

1. Jeff Bezos' mom, Jackie, was a teenager when she had him in January 1964. She had recently married Cuban immigrant Mike Bezos, who adopted Jeff. Jeff didn't learn that Mike wasn't his real father until he was ten, but says he was more fazed about learning he needed to get glasses than he was about the news.

2. He was a smart and resourceful child. When he was a toddler, he took apart his crib with a screwdriver because he wanted to sleep in a bed.

3. Between 4 and 16, Bezos spent summers on his grandparents' ranch in Texas, doing farm work like repairing windmills and castrating bulls.

4. His grandfather, Preston Gise, was a huge inspiration for Bezos, and helped kindle his passion for intellectual pursuits. At a commencement address in 2010, Bezos said

that Gise taught him that "it's harder to be kind than clever."

5. Growing up, Bezos loved Star Trek, watching re-runs after school almost every day. Early on, he thought about calling Amazon MakeItSo.com in reference to a famous line from Star Trek.

6. After spending a miserable summer working at McDonald's as a teen, Bezos and his girlfriend started the DREAM Institute, a ten day summer-camp for kids. They charged $600 per kid, but managed to sign-up six students. The 'Lord of the Rings' series made the required reading list.

7. He eventually went to college at Princeton and majored in computer science. Upon graduation, he turned down job offers from Intel and Bell Labs to join a startup called Fitel.

8. After Fitel, he got a job at Bankers Trust, and eventually at hedge fund firm D.E. Shaw. He became a senior vice president after only four years.

9. Meanwhile, Bezos took ballroom dancing classes as part of a scheme to increase his "women flow." Like Wall Streeters have a process for increasing their "deal flow," Bezos thought about meeting girls analytically.

10. He eventually married MacKenzie Tuttle, a D.E. Shaw a research associate, in 1993. She's now a novelist.

11 .In 1994, Bezos read that the Web had grown 2,300% in one year. This number astounded him, and he decided he needed to find some way to take advantage of its rapid growth. He made a list of 20 possible product categories to sell online, and decided that books were the best option.

12. Bezos decided to leave D.E. Shaw even though he had a great job. "When you are in the thick of things, you can get confused by small stuff," he said later. "I knew when I was eighty that I would never, for example, think about why I walked away from my 1994 Wall Street bonus right in the middle of the year at the worst possible time.

That kind of thing just isn't something you worry about when you're eighty years old. At the same time, I knew that I might sincerely regret not having participated in this thing called the Internet that I thought was going to be a revolutionizing event. When I thought about it that way… it was incredibly easy to make the decision."

13. And so Amazon was born. MacKenzie and Jeff flew to Texas to borrow a car from his father, and then they drove to Seattle. Bezos was making revenue projections in the passenger seat the whole way, though the couple did stop to watch the sunrise over the Grand Canyon.

14. In the early days, a bell would ring in the office every time someone made a purchase, and everyone would gather around to see if they knew the customer. It only took a few weeks before it was ringing so often the they had to make it stop.

15. Learn more about some of Amazon's early employees here.

16. Jeff Bezos was a demanding boss and could explode at employees. Rumor has it, he hired a leadership coach to help him tone it down.

17. In 1998, Bezos also became an early investor in Google. He invested $250,000, which was about 3.3 million shares when the company IPO'd in 2004 — or over $280 million. (He hasn't revealed whether or not he kept any of his stock after the IPO).

18. Today, Bezos is worth about $30 billion.

19. What does Bezos do with all his money? In 2012, he donated $2.5 million to defend gay marriage in Washington.

20. Bezos has also donated $42 million and part of his land in Texas to the construction of The Clock Of The Long Now, an underground clock designed to work for 10,000 years.

21. In August 2013, Bezos bought The Washington Post for $250 million.

22. He funds a private space company called Blue Origin, which is working on developing technology for private space travel.

23. In 2003, Jeff Bezos almost died in a helicopter crash while scouting a site for the company's test-launch facility in the boondocks of west Texas.

24. The company currently employees about 300 people and it's in the process of getting one of its rocket engines certified for use.

25. Late 2013, Bezos made a splash by announcing on "60 Minutes" that Amazon was working on drones that could deliver orders in 30 minutes.

26. He owns a house on Lake Washington, as well as a $24.25 million Beverly Hills estate.

27. It's been a big year for Amazon. The company released a TV streaming box as well as smartphone.

MARK ZUCKERBERG

On May 14th, 1984, Mark Zuckerberg was born in the small White Plains town, in New York. He was the fourth child of Karen Kempner and Edward Zuckerberg, who already had three girls. This was how all began... Currently Mark is only 32 and his net worth by year 2016 was estimated at $54.8 billion. But the fact that he is one of the youngest billionaires is the less interesting one. The cool stuff here is actually his start up story, telling how a kid became the founder and later the manager of one of the most influential websites on Earth. Below is the amazing story of this young entrepreneur and his creation – Facebook.

Early Days

Mark began writing software and using computers when he was in middle school. His coding experience began with learning Atari basic programming, with the help of his father Edward Zuckerberg. But he was learning so fast, that daddy needed to hire a professional developer to tutor him. David Newman was the man, who was given the task to mentor the young Mark. It was a tough task for the teacher, because the student was developing his skills so quickly, that Newman experienced serious difficulties to stay ahead of him. At high school Mark excelled in his classes.

He won prizes in astronomy, physics, and mathematics. While he was still in high school, he took a college graduate program in computer programming. He built a program called Zucknet where the computer at home could communicate with his father's computer at his dental practice. He also used his creativity to build computer games often out of ideas his friends would draw for him. When he eventually went to go to college, he claimed to be able to read and write in Latin, French, Hebrew, English and Greek. His overall knowledge and intelligence helped him excel at college, where he would often recite poems such as the epic 'The Iliad'.

In college (The Harvard University) he was already known as a "programming prodigy" due to the work he had done in high school. There he wrote a program he called CourseMatch that helped students make decisions about the courses they wanted to take based upon the choices of others.

In college, the students have books called "Facebooks." They have the pictures and names of people that lived in the student dorms. Mark built a website that randomly showed two pictures of males and two of females on it. People that visited the site had to choose which person was hotter. This site went up over one weekend and it was called Facemash (actually this was the first name of Facebook). It was built 'just for fun' but it became so popular, that the college shut it down because of its popularity. First it caused the Harvard's servers to crash (because of the heavy load it caused) and this caused problems for the student, who wanted to use the Internet. Also, some students didn't like the idea of their pictures being used without permission and Zuckerberg was forced to apologize for his actions.

In 2004 he began writing a new website which he called TheFacebook , working on thefacebook.com domain (the second name of the network). He had several students helping him with TheFacebook including Eduardo Saverin, Andrew McCollum, Chris Hughes and Dustin Moskovitz, who are actually the other 4 co-founders of the site. The site was initially just a Harvard site but soon expanded to other colleges and universities. Mark and friends decided to spread the idea and many other universities were included in the network. The social project started gaining momentum really fast and Zuckerberg decided to drop out of college and dedicate his time entirely to the site.

He and his team moved in a small house in Palo Alto, which became the office of the young enterprise. By 2005 "TheFacebook" was known just as Facebook. The site opened up to anyone over age 13 in 2006. By 2007 the site had over 100,000 businesses listing their companies on Facebook and creating pages. By 2011 it became the largest digital photograph host and had over 350 million accessing the site over mobile phones.

On May 18th 2012 Facebook made its IPO (initial public offering), offering 421 million shares to private investors at the price of $38. This set the value of the whole company at $104 billion, which made Facebook the biggest business going public till then. Almost everybody wanted to buy a piece of the booming social miracle, so rising almost $16 billion from the market was like a walk in the park.

However, things didn't went well for investors. Just two weeks after the IPO, the market price of the shares fell dramatically by 27% to $27.72 per share. During the next months the price went down even further, reaching level around $19 . All this didn't make investors really happy, some of whom lost around 50% of their investments for a few months. More than 40 lawsuits were filled the first week after the IPO. The price has recovered in 2013 and currently it's around $41.

Mark Zuckerberg was named to the 100 wealthiest and most influential people in the world list put out by Time magazine in 2010. Zuckerberg, who is also Jewish, is listed as one of the most influential Jews in the world as well. His net worth is estimated at $54.78 billion in 2016 and currently he is the CEO (Chief Executive Officer) of the social company. There is no doubt that Facebook has changed the way we communicate on-line and today it remains a very popular site thanks to this young entrepreneur.

LARRY ELLISON

You may not have heard about Larry Ellison but you may certainly have heard about Oracle. This multi-billion software company was started by this billionaire. Ellison is currently the 5th richest person in the world with a net worth of $49 Billion. You may not know this, but the movie Iron Man was based on the life of this man. The next time you watch the Iron Man movies again, try and spot Oracle signs and building. You may also spot him doing a cameo appearance in Iron Man 2.

A Difficult Childhood

Born in the Bronx, Larry Ellison had a difficult childhood. His mother was only 19 years old and single, so she gave Larry to his uncle and aunt to raise. Moved to Chicago, Ellison grew up in a small two-bedroom apartment. He found out that he was adopted when he was 12 years old. Around this time, his adoptive father lost his business due to the Depression and started working as an auditor. Rebellious and independent-minded, Larry Ellison showed an aptitude for science.

After dropping out of the University of Illinois, he transferred to the University of Chicago before dropping out a semester later. This constant changing of schools caused his adoptive father to believe that Larry would never learn anything with his life. Instead, Ellison began to learn about computer programming. After saving up enough money for gas, Ellison decided to move to Berkeley, California. He switched jobs frequently for eight years before working on a mainframe system with Amdahl Corporation.

The Creation of Oracle

By 1977, Ellison decided to create a company with his co-workers, Ed Oates and Robert Miner. They named their new business, Software Development Labs. After reading a paper about a Structured Query Language, Larry started working on a range of new projects.

His company was hired by the CIA to build Oracle. They completed the project one year early and used the remaining time to figure out commercial applications. This relational database management system (RDBMS) was named Oracle as well. By 1981, IBM chose to adopt Oracle and Oracle's sales doubled. For the next seven years, sales doubled annually. This success with Oracle led to Ellison renaming the business Oracle Company.

Oracle Goes Public

In 1986, Oracle finally went public. The initial public offering served to raise $31.5 million. By 1990, the company reported its first losses due to years of overstated revenue. This caused the market capitalization to drop by

80 percent and pushed Oracle to the edge of bankruptcy. To keep the company solvent, Ellison fired top level employees and brought in more experienced managers. Larry Ellison used this change as an opportunity to step back from management and focus more on product development. Oracle 7 was released in 1992 and the company's fortunes started to improve.

Throughout the 1990s, a range of financial institutions, retail businesses and automobile companies turned to Oracle for database programs. Due to this, Ellison was encouraged to find business applications for Oracle online. As ecommerce sites grew, net profits increased. In one quarter in 2000, the profits jumped by 76 percent. This caused Larry Ellison to surpass Bill Gates as the world's richest man at that time.

Starting in 2004, Ellison worked to increase Oracle's market share by acquiring a range of other companies. After purchasing Sun Microsystems in 2009, Oracle became the biggest software company in the world. Larry Ellison has served as the president of Oracle from 1978 to 1996 and brief time periods as the Chairman of the Board. Since the early beginnings of Oracle, Ellison has been the company's only CEO.

MICHAEL BLOOMBERG

Michael Bloomberg is most famous today as the post 9/11 mayor of New York City, but he began his career with the reputable Wall Street firm Salomon Brothers and quickly rose in the ranks until he was a rising star buying and selling blocks of stock sold by large institutions.

But Bloomberg's star only shot so high at Salomon. He excelled as a trader, and he was made partner and then given responsibility for all equities.But in 1978, just as abruptly, he was demoted to run the information technology division of the company, where he was still stationed in 1981 when Salomon Brothers decided to merge with the commodity trading firm Phibro. Bloomberg was given a pat on the back and a severance check of $10 million.

The company he'd worked for since graduating from Harvard Business School,the company he has said he would never have left was letting him go. Bloomberg was thirty-nine years old when this happened and couldn't imagine going to work for a different Wall Street firm.He took a chunk of the $10 million and created a business that merged the two skills he had developed at Salomon Brothers knowledge of the securities and investment business, and of the technologies that assisted in the deals.

When it came to knowing the relative value of one security versus another, most of Wall Street in 1981 had pretty much remained where it was when I began as a clerk back in the mid-1960s: a bunch of guys using No. 2 pencils, chronicling the seat-of-the-pants guesses of too many bored trades," Bloomberg has written about the state of investment data at the time.

Bloomberg imagined that he could build a system that took information about a mass of different investment types (stocks, bonds, currencies) and reveal a firm's position and show what was moving where so traders could see investment opportunities previously hidden by too much (and too inaccessible) data. Bloomberg hired four former Salomon people, including his Performer complement Tom Secunda, who wrote the first analytics programs, and got to work selling and dealing the as yet-uninvented Bloomberg terminal.

Merrill Lynch's Capital Markets Division was the first prospect. As Bloomberg tells it, he went alone to a meeting with Ed Moriarty, he division head, and pitched the nonexistent product to him and his team as if it were established.

When Bloomberg finished, Moriarty turned to Hank Alexander, the head of his software department, and asked his opinion. Alexander said he thought they should build it themselves,a not uncommon response in the "build it here" world of investment banking technology.

When Moriarty asked how long it would take, Alexander reportedly said, "Well, if you don't give us anything new to do we'll be able to start in six months." With that opening, Bloomberg said, "I'll get it done in six months and if you don't like it, you don't have to pay for it."

Bloomberg and his team had little more than an idea of what could help the traders at one of the country's most respected commercial banks. But he made a deal on that idea as if it existed already. Bloomberg used his persuasive capacity to sell the vision and then he went to work building a custom terminal that brought in proprietary data and analytics.

"It wasn't elegant," he said of the first Bloomberg terminal they delivered. "It was laughably simplistic by today's standards. But we did it, and it worked."Michael Bloomberg, 88% owner of Bloomberg L.P and current Mayor of New York City, was born in 1942, February 14, at St. Elizabeth's Hospital in the Brighton neighborhood of Boston to middle class parents.

He completed his Bachelor of Science degree in electrical engineering from Johns Hopkins University and received MBA degree from Harvard Business School. He started his life as a trader with Salomon Brothers on Wall Street and they became partner in 1972. He leant how technological innovation plays an important role making a business successful. In 1981, he was fired with $10 million severance payout with which he opened a financial data and communications company called Innovative Market System.

The company was renamed as Bloomberg LP in 1986. Today, Bloomberg L.P has more than 165,000 subscribers across the world and it gradually expanded and launched news service, Bloomberg Business T.V, Bloomberg business radio, Bloomberg Internet and various public operations. In 1997, Bloomberg published his autobiography named 'Bloomberg by Bloomberg'. In 2001, he resigned from his position to become a Mayor of New York.

Philanthropic Work:

He has donated over $300 million to Johns Hopkins University, where he was Chairman of the board since 2002. In 2006, he donated to Centers for Disease Control and Prevention, World Lung Foundation and the World Health Organization, Johns Hopkins Bloomberg School for Public Health and to the Campaign for Tobacco-Free Kids.

He has contributed $138 million in 2004, $144 million in 2005, $165 million in 2006, and $205 million in 2007 to 'Chronicle of Philanthropy' through Bloomberg Family Foundation. In 2008, he, along with Bill Gates, donated to the Government to get control over tobacco. In 2009, he has donated $254 million to 1400 non-profit organizations.

According to Forbes Magazine 2010, Michael Bloomberg is the world's 23rd richest with net worth $18 billion in fortune.

RICHARD BRANSON

Richard Branson is the British business magnate and investor. He is the founder of Virgin Group and has owned more than 400 companies.

He is the only entrepreneur to build eight separate billion dollar companies in eight different industries and his net worth is $5 billion. Known for his daredevil personality, Richard Branson's business venture included Virgin Megastores, Virgin Mobiles, Virgin Airlines and Virgin Galactic; the Virgin Spaceflight Company.

There is a very interesting story behind the start of Virgin Airlines, have a look at the success story of Richard Branson.

The Success Journey of Richard Branson

Dropout from School and Started Student Magazine.

Having no interest in studies, he dropped out from school at the age of 16 years to start magazine named "Student." It was a mail-order record business. He made a quick buck by selling advertisements to local businesses.

He writes about the education in his new book, Like a Virgin: Secrets They Won't Teach You at Business School.

Had I pursued my education long enough to learn all the conventional dos and don'ts of starting a business I often wonder how different my life and career might have been. - Richard Branson

Founded Virgin Records

He started selling mail records to the students who bought the magazine. His idea worked so well that within one year, he opened his own recording label and recording studio and named it as "Virgin Records."

His record company witnessed a huge success as high profile performers like the Rolling Stones and Sex Pistols signed under the label. Branson became millionaire by the age of 23. Nowadays, his Virgin Records is popularly known as Virgin Megastore.

How he Started Virgin Airlines

Branson was in his late twenties and was going to Virgin Island to meet his girlfriend. At the airport, his final flight to the Virgin Island was cancelled because of some reason. It was the last flight of the day and he was really desperate to go there, but he can't unless he chartered a private airplane that can take him to the Virgin Island.

But he didn't have that much money and at that time, an idea clicked in his mind. He picked up a small blackboard and wrote "Virgin Airlines $29" on it. He sold the tickets to the people who too wanted to go to the Virgin Island.

He used that money to pay for the chartered plane and everybody reached their destination with the help of "VIRGIN AIRLINES." And after that, he acted upon that idea to make it the real business and founded Virgin Airlines.

Today he owns more than 400 companies including many ventures, businesses, expeditions and various other businesses. But his educational qualification is too small for all this.

He had never flown any plane and didn't know anything about planes, but he started airlines anyway. Actually he was never prepared for the things he did in his life but he took the initiative anyway to make that happen and guess what? He was successful at every step!

LI KA-SHING

Li Ka-shing was born on 13th of June 1928 in the South Eastern coastal city of Chiu Chow, China. He is known as the most influential business man in East Asia and Hong Kong.

His father, the head of a primary school, died when Li Ka-Shing was only 12. Soon the responsibility of shouldering family came upon a him. Shing started his life selling watch bands at local market and bus stops and ended up became wholesaler at the age of 17. Years of dedication and hardwork facilitated him to come out from engrossed poverty and start his own company Cheung Kong Industries by 1950. Ever since, he has successfully expanded his business in more than 40 countries across the world.

According to reports of 2008, he was the 11th richest business man with net worth at $26.4 billion. He has received Honorary Doctorate from University of Cambridge, University Of Calgary, Hong Kong University Of Science And Technology, Chinese University of Hong Kong, City University of Hong Kong, University of Hong Kong, The Open University Of Hong Kong, Peking University. In 2006, September 5, he was honored with "Malcolm S. Forbes Lifetime Achievement Award" by Forbes family.

Philanthropic work:

In 2002, The Li Ka Shing donated US$11.5 million to Singapore Management University after which The Li Ka Shing Library was named after to show honor towards him. In 2004, he contributed US$3 million for Indian Ocean Earth Quake.

In 2005, he has contributed US$128 million to the Faculty of Medicine, University of Hong Kong. The same year, he donated US$40 million to the University of California, Berkeley.

In 2006, he pledged $10 billion for charity work throughout the world.

In 2007, Li Ka-Shing donated S$100 million to the Lee Kuan Yew School of Public Policy in the National University of Singapore. He has also given CAD$25 million to St. Michael's Hospital in Toronto. In the 2008 Sichuan earthquake, he donated US$3.85 million.

GEORGE SOROS

He is a self-made billionaire known for his investment savvy and his vast body of philanthropic work. Born in Budapest, Hungary, on August 12, 1930, George Soros survived Nazi occupation followed by Communist-rule in Hungary in the mid-1940s and emigrated to London. There he studied economics and after earning his degree, moved to New York City in 1956, where he entered a life of finance. He began his renowned philanthropic efforts in 1979, and as of 2012 his lifetime giving amounts to more than $7 billion via his Open Society Foundations.

Early Years

George Soros was born Gyorgy Schwartz in Budapest, Hungary, on August 12, 1930 to parents Tividar and Erzebat Schwartz. To avoid growing anti-Semite persecution, his father changed their surname to Soros in 1936. As a teenager, he survived the Nazi invasion and occupation of Hungary in 1944.

A few years after WWII ended, Soros emigrated from the then-Communist-dominated Hungary in 1947 and made his way to England. There, at the London School of Economics, Soros began studying Karl Popper's The Open Society and Its Enemies, which explores the philosophy of science and serves as Popper's critique of totalitarianism.

The essential lesson the book imparted to Soros was that no ideology owns the truth, and that societies can flourish only when they operate freely and openly and maintain respect for individual rights—thoughts that would deeply influence Soros for the rest of his life.

Soros graduated in 1952, and in September 1956 he sailed to New York and took a job at Wall Street brokerage firm F.M. Mayer. After working for a few more firms, in 1973 Soros set up his own hedge fund (the Soros Fund, soon after renamed the Quantum Fund and later the Quantum Fund Endowment) with $12 million from investors. The fund, with Soros at the helm, found massive success through its various iterations, and as of September 2015, Soros, at 85 years of age, was deemed as the 21st richest person in the world, with an estimated net worth of $26 billion.

Activities and Controversies

George Soros began his philanthropic activity in 1979, and he established the Open Society Foundation in 1984. The foundation funds a range of global initiatives "to advance justice, education, public health, business development and independent media." The causes Soros helps with his foundation are numerous (the foundation's list of activities goes on for 500 pages), but they include aiding in regions struck by natural disaster, establishing after-school programs in New York City, funding the arts, lending financial assistance to the Russian university system, fighting disease and combating "brain drain" in Eastern Europe.

While a towering figure in the philanthropic world, George Soros is also a provocative figure. Among his controversial positions are that he supports altering the United States' "war on drugs" to avoid the current extent of criminalization, he was involved in and profited heavily from the U.K. currency crisis of 1992 (dubbed Black Wednesday), he has written several books on the looming collapse of the financial markets (and certain observers accuse him of manipulating the markets to reach his ends) and he has said that policies of the United States and Israel have given rise to global anti-Semitism.

Controversial or beloved, with his countless organizations (through which he shapes public policy and undertakes vast humanitarian projects), financial empire and the 12 books he's written on subjects ranging from the war on terror to global capitalism, George Soros is an influential figure and a giant in finance and the realm of philanthropy.

PHIL KNIGHT

He began his career like most ordinary college grads: no money, no clear direction and what looked like a lifetime at a desk job as an accountant. What transpired instead was one of the greatest stories of American entrepreneurship and a $100 billion sportswear giant. This is the story of Nike Co-founder Phil Knight, who turned his crazy idea into reality. The 78-year-old is telling the story behind Nike for the first time in his new memoir, "Shoe Dog."

The idea for the athletic apparel giant "came from running track at Hayward Field in Oregon and out of the classroom at Stanford business school," Knight said.

A self-described "average mid-distance runner" on the track team, Phil "Buck" Knight watched as his track coach at University of Oregon, Bill Bowerman, tinkered with athletes' running shoes and the immediate impact it made on their performance.

Combine that with a paper he wrote at Stanford on why shoes should be manufactured out of Japan (instead of Germany), where the labor was cheaper, and his crazy idea was born. First called Blue Ribbon Sports, Knight's business began on a whim, when he convinced a group of Japanese businessmen to export their popular Tiger sneakers to the United States and grant him exclusivity in selling them.

After selling Tigers out of the trunk of his car, Knight saw the demand was there. So he ordered more sneakers from Japan. And more. Until he had to hire additional people to keep up with the growing demand. It wasn't always a smooth ride. Knight's shipments from Japan were rarely on time, and he frequently faced major financing problems. Despite Knight doubling his sales constantly, banks were reluctant to provide the loans needed, and two banks ultimately dropped him as a customer.

When trouble began with the Japanese company over their exclusivity agreement, Knight was forced to break from the factory. Blue Ribbon Sports was essentially starting over. Knight and his 45 employees at the time had to find new factories to produce their shoes, and even create a new name for the company.

Knight originally wanted to call the company "Dimension Six," something he was teased about later on. "Just think where we'd be if I picked that name," he said. "When Jeff Johnson came up with Nike, I didn't know if I liked it too much, but it's better than the other names. It turned out pretty good," he added.

After years of strong growth but with struggles to stay in the black, Knight and his team decided in December of 1980 to finally take Nike public. "We were concerned about losing control," said Knight, who added that ultimately, it was one of the best things the company ever did.

Immediately, Knight's ownership in shares made him worth $178 million. Today, Forbes estimates his net worth at more than $25 billion, making him the 24th richest person in the United States. Nike has more than $30 billion in sales, it represents the top athletes in the world and it has achieved a truly global footprint.

Knight's advice to other entrepreneurs? "Be prepared for a lot of hardship and unexpected setbacks. For me, there was nothing that I would have rather done."

In June, Knight is handing the baton to Nike CEO Mark Parker, who will take over as chairman of the board. "I'm excited about the future of Nike," Knight said. "I think a great growth period lies ahead."

JACK MA

Alibaba became an international sensation after its IPO garnered an offering which had never been heard before in the history of New York Stock exchange. The brain behind this e-commerce company is Jack Ma who rose from modest beginnings to heights of success. With a net worth of $25 billion, Jack is touted as the richest man in the Republic of China.

Read on to learn more about the life and ordeals of the business conglomerate.

1. Born to traditional musician-storyteller parents on October 15, 1964 in Hangzhou, China, Jack Ma was the second child in the family. Jack and his two siblings – an elder brother and a younger sister – had a modest upbringing. During their childhood, Communism was at peak in the country and the residents had little or no contact with the Western World.

2. The billionaire had a fighting streak in him since childhood; he would take on opponents who were much stronger than him. In the book 'Alibaba', which chronicles the journey of the Alibaba.com, Ma recalls "I was never afraid of opponents who were bigger than I." The scrawny kid however like others harbored many hobbies. His favorite pastime was collecting crickets; such was his

interest in the insects that he could identify them based on the sound they made.

3. The year 1972 was a milestone in the history of Hangzhou as US President Richard Nixon visited the city. Following the visit, tourism boomed in the city and the spirited Ma made the most of the opportunity. He would work as a tourist guide in exchange for lessons in English. Apparently he also befriended one of the tourists and the two continued correspondence. His pen pal named him Jack as he found Ma's original name a little too difficult to pronounce.

4. Hailing from a family of modest means, the only way out for Jack was higher studies. He failed the University entrance examinations twice but his perseverance paid off in the third attempt. He enrolled at the Hangzhou Teacher's Institute, from where he obtained a bachelor's degree in English in the year 1988.

5. Ma went through numerous rejections that even included one from the fast food chain KFC, before landing a teaching job. The local university paid him only $12 per month but Jack had a natural flair for teaching and was quite popular among his students.

6. In 1995, Jack who had recently ventured into the translation business had to visit the US. During the trip, where he had to collect the remuneration for one of the Chinese firms, he had his first try with the internet. It is

said that the lack of results displaying Chinese beers when he searched for them online, inspired him to create an internet company for the nation.

7. Jack's maiden attempts at hosting a Chinese website did not see the daylight owing to lack of funding, among other reasons. However even a second failed attempt did not deter him from his goals. He continued with determination and finally his efforts bore fruition when he was able to convince 17 of his friends to invest in 'Alibaba'. The China-based business-to-business marketplace site served as a portal for exporters to list their products. Customers can compare prices and place orders directly to the dealer of their choice through the portal.

8. The popularity of the website soared quickly as Ma continued to improvise the services offered to visitors. By 1999, Alibaba was able to garner funding worth $5 million from Goldman Sachs and another $20 million from SoftBank, a Japanese telecom giant. Ma was an efficient leader and motivated his small but close-knit team to deliver the best. At one team gathering Ma said to his employees, "We will make it because we are young and we never, never give up."

9. The entrepreneur is nothing like the conventional corporate leaders and encourages a dash of humor at the work place. To mark the celebration of the company breaking even and registering their first profit, he presented a can of Silly String to the employees. In the early 2000s

Jack decided to go head first into competition with rival eBay, and thus came into being Taobao. Apparently Jack's idea of revving up the energy levels of the team working on Taobao was to do handstands during the breaks.

10. Their competition with eBay in China received a great boost after internet giant Yahoo invested a billion dollars in the former. The deal was a win-win for both the parties— Yahoo, which now owned 40 percent shares in Alibaba earned a whopping 10 billion dollars in the IPO alone.

11. Year 2013 was monumental in the life of Jack as well as for his brainchild company. Though he signed off his responsibilities as the CEO of the company, he continued to don the role of executive chairman. The same year in September the company went public and the $150 billion IPO was a record breaker; no other US-listed company had ever received such a whopping offer in the history of NYSE. "Today what we got is not money. What we got is the trust from the people," Ma told CNBC after the IPO. The successful IPO sky-rocketed Ma's assets and his net worth stood at a staggering value of $25 billion.

12. The employees were ecstatic at the IPO's success and a grand party was organized at the Hangzhou headquarters of the company. Addressing his employees during a press conference Jack said that he hopes they use their newfound wealth to become "a batch of genuinely noble people, a batch of people who are able to help others, and who are kind and happy."

13. Despite becoming the wealthiest man in China, Ma remains the down to earth person he was, before his fame reached far and wide. The multibillionaire, according to his friend Xiao-Ping Chen is pretty much the same, "I don't think he has changed much, he is still that old style." He still pursues his hobbies of reading and writing Kung fu fiction, playing poker, meditating and practicing tai chi among others. He associated with another proponent of tai chi, Jet Li in order to raise awareness regarding the martial arts form. According to sources a trainer always escorts Jack while he is travelling.

14. The business magnate is also a crusader of environmental conservation and is a member of the global board of The Nature Conservancy. He presented his views at the Clinton Global Initiative in 2015 and also made a hefty contribution to build the 27,000-acre nature reserve in China.

15. Ma is a private person and likes to keep his family away from the spotlight. The conglomerate is married to Zhang Ying, whom he met after graduation in the late 1980s. Ying who is a teacher by profession says, "[He] is not a handsome man, but I fell for him because he can do a lot of things handsome men cannot do." The couple has a daughter and a son.

16. Though Jack believes in leading a modest life, he indulges in a few splurges once in a while. The business

tycoon owns a Gulfstream G550, the business jet aircraft, worth a whopping cost of $49.7 million.

17. The entrepreneur commands no less respect and love than a celebrity in his country, where people gather in huge numbers to listen to him.

18. A connoisseur of new talent, Alibaba organizes a talent show every year wherein even Jack puts up an act. During one of the functions, he turned up as a punk rocker before an audience of 20,000 people.

19. According to sources in the company, Jack was in a café in San Francisco when he coined the name 'Alibaba' for his business. The company's meteoric rise is in a way similar to the folk tale of Ali Baba and the Forty Thieves where a password unlocked a cave filled with riches.

MUKESH AMBANI

The richest person in India and MD and chairman of Reliance Industries, the largest Indian private sector enterprise, Mukesh Dhirubhai Ambani is a worthy example of business tycoons carrying forward legacy.

The elder son of Legendary business leader late Dhirubhai Ambani, he has played a pivotal role in taking Reliance Industries Limited to zenith of success in his illustrious career. Despite the steep competition from rival tycoons like Tatas and Birlas and allegations of business malpractice, Mukesh Ambani continues his success in various spheres of business. Along with the tremendous growth of his Fortune Global 500 company, Mukesh Ambani has often hogged headlines for his lavish lifestyle and diversification into other industries.

Located in South Mumbai, his skyscraper home Antilia has been rated as the world's costliest residential property by prestigious Forbes Magazine. He held the position of the richest Indian for 6 years.

Early Life

Mukesh Ambani was born on April 19th 1957 to Indian Business Legend Dhirubhai Ambani and his wife Kokilaben Ambani. He has three siblings, one younger brother, Anil Ambani and two sisters, Deepti Salgaocar and

Nina Kothari. The family lived in a modest two bedroom apartment till the late 1970s in Bhuleshwar, Mumbai.

Education

Mukesh attended the Hill Grange High School at Peddar Road in Mumbai where he was a classmate of Anand Jain, who is his close associate now. His brother also attended the same school as him.

After completing his high school in Mumbai he got a BE Degree in Chemical Engineering from Institute of Chemical technology at Matunga. He also started his MBA in Stanford University but he had to discontinue his studies to assist his father in the family startup company, Reliance, which was growing fast at the time. After joining the business, Mukesh Ambani played a pivotal role in growing the business legacy and diversified into new sectors.

Under his leadership, Reliance Industries made a foray into sectors like petroleum refining, petrochemicals and gas exploration. He also set up Reliance Infocomm Limited (presently Reliance Communications Limited).

Career

In 2010, Mukesh Ambani set up the biggest grassroots petroleum refinery plant in Jamnagar. With his initiative, manufacturing capacity of Reliance's Petrochemicals has grown substantially as per industry sources. The company has also become a leading player in the retail sector, under his leadership and endeavors. With his successful and enviable business career, Mukesh Ambani has gone through some turbulent times, too.

His rift with sibling Anil Ambani, another business tycoon and chairman of Reliance ADA Group, hogged media attention post the demise of their father. In recent times, the NDA government slammed a $579 million fine on RIL for gas production shortfall. Mukesh Ambani faced hurdles in the form of business malpractice allegations too. His detractors, including AAP founder Arvind Kejriwal accused him of interfering in the governance of the country. RIL as well as Mukesh Ambani himself have denied the allegations strongly.

The company has also resorted to legal actions over the controversy. The numerous acquisitions made by RIL, the acknowledgement from leading business entities, and his firm hold on the throne of India's richest person have not made Mukesh Ambani complacent. Reliance Jio Infocomm, his telecom arm is all set to roll out 4G services in alliance with his sibling Anil Ambani's company.

" Essentially, whoever is successful, whoever is going to do things that make a difference, is going to be talked about.'
– Mukesh Dhirubhai Ambani

Mukesh Ambani announced a few months back that Reliance Jio Infocomm will launch 4G services in commercial capacity in 2015, incurring a whopping 70,000 core investment in India. It will use the pan-India BWA spectrum for the 4G service rollout, which will cover almost 90 per cent of urban regions and more than 215,000 villages. It is being deemed as an aggressive move by industry analysts at a time when telecom companies are vying for 4G dominance.

Life

Ambani family

Mukesh Ambani is married to Nita Ambani and they have three children. Two sons, Akash and Anant and a daughter Isha. He lives with his family in Mumbai in an apartment of a private 27 storey building named Antilia. His residence is known to be one of the most expensive residential places ever built in the world. It is currently valued at over $ 1 billion.

Mukesh Ambani is the Chairman and Managing Director of Reliance Industries Limited, India's Largest Private Sector Company. He is the elder son of the legendry businessman late Dhirubhai Ambani. Mukesh Ambani has the following business interests: Petrochemicals, Petroleum Refining and Marketing, Oil and Gas exploration and production, Textiles, Retail and SEZs. Forbes (2009) list of the world's billionaires named him the richest man in India and the 7th richest man in the world, having a net worth of $ 19.5 Billion.

Mukesh Ambani was born on April 19, Year 1957. He studied at Abaay Morischa School in Mumbai. He completed his chemical engineering from University of Mumbai. He went to Stanford University in the US for his Masters in Business Administration (MBA), but did not complete the course as he had to come back to join the family business.

In the year 1981 Mukesh Ambani joined Reliance. He was the key man at the time of the company's backward integration from textiles into polyester fibres, and then into petrochemicals. He established a number of world class manufacturing facilities to take the company's petrochemical manufacturing capabilities to a new level. Mukesh Ambani conceptualized and created the largest grass roots petroleum refinery in the world at Jamnagar, Gujrat, India. The refinery has a capacity of 33 million tonnes per year.

Mukesh Ambani helped to set up one of the world's leading telecommunications Companies, Reliance Communications, earlier known as Reliance Infocom. Reliance Communications went to younger brother Anil Ambani of ADAG, after the business empire got split in the year 2005.

Mukesh Ambani entered into the organized retail sector with Reliance Retail, opening hundreds of stores across several states. The stores serve diverse consumer needs and operate under various names such as Reliance Fresh,

Reliance Mart and Reliance Digital. Mukesh Ambani owns the Indian Premier League (IPL) Cricket Team, Mumbai Indians. He brought the team for $111.9 million.

Mukesh Ambani gifted his Wife Nita Ambani a $60 million Airbus Plane on her 44th birthday. The customized jet had a master bedroom, fancy showers, game consoles, music systems, satellite TV, and wireless communication.

Mukesh Ambani is building a 27 story house called Antilla, at Altamount Road, Mumbai. The 400000 square feet home will have 6 levels of car parking, 3 helipads, 4 levels of open gardens, 2 levels of health club, home theatre, swimming pools, a ball room with the ceiling covered with crystalchandeliers, 9 elevators, an ice room and much more. The cost of the new home may touch $ 2 billion.

PAUL ALLEN

He was born on January 21, 1953 in Seattle, Washington. He is famously known for co-founding Microsoft along with Bill Gates. He has around $15 billion of wealth as of 2013 and is one of the Top 60 richest people in the world. He met Bill Gates at Lakeside School, when he was 14 and Gates was 12. They both had a common passion for computers. In 1973, Allen got a 100 percentile score in SAT and joined Washington State University. But after two years he dropped out to work as a programmer for a computer company Honeywell situated in Boston.

After some time there he planned to start his own company, so he asked his friend Gates to join him. Gates dropped out of Harvard to join Allen and open a new company which they named Microsoft. This was the time when the wave of personal computer systems had hit America. Allen and Gates decided to design a new software that would run on these new PC's. They started by supplying the Microsoft BASIC software they had created to emerging companies like Commodore and Apple.

Allen got hold of a big contract from IBM by promising to give them a DOS (Disc Operating System) software. But Microsoft had not designed such a complicated software yet. So Allen went on to make the most profitable move that Microsoft has ever made. He went ahead in buying a software called QDOS (Quick and Dirty Operating System) written by Tim Paterson.

Then Allen and Gates re-invented the QDOS and made it the MS-DOS (Microsoft Disk Operating System). The MS-DOS software was installed on the Intel 8088-based IBM Personal computer which began selling in 1981. This new PC revolutionised computing in America. Soon Allen and Gates went on to become millionaires as they received royalty for every PC that was sold. But tragedy struck Allen when he was diagnosed with a cancer named Hodgkin's lymphoma in 1982.

He fully recovered only after months of radiation therapy. But after his disease had recovered he began to distance himself from Microsoft and decided to try his hand at new innovations and research.

Career Highlights

At the age of 30, Allen was a billionaire thanks to the increasing stock price of Microsoft. Now he concentrated on investing in start-ups and started the company called Vulcan Ventures in 1986.

He invested in diverse sectors like online directories, hardware and wireless communications. By 1998 he had acquired more than 30 companies under him. By 1999 he had over $25 billion holdings in just the cable and internet business. He remained on the Board of directors in

Microsoft till November 2000. As of 2013 he still reportedly owns approximately 138 million shares of Microsoft. His business acumen has been the key behind his immense success as an entrepreneur.

His strategic investments have made Microsoft what it is today. From dropping out of college to start a own company, he has journeyed to become one of the most respected business advisors on the planet. He has also played a huge hand in promoting science and technology by giving away more than $300 million in 2011 itself. He will always be remembered for his successful execution of high-risk strategies which has helped him create billions of dollars in profit for his company.

Allen also has interest in sports. He possesses three professional sports teams: the Portland Trail Blazers of the National Basketball Association that he acquired in 1988 for $77 million, the Seattle Seahawks of the National Football League that he bought in 1997 and the Seattle Sounders FC franchise that started playing in 2009.

According to Forbes 2011, Allen is the 57th richest person in the world with the fortune worth $13.3 billion.

AL-WALEED BIN TALAL

Prince Alwaleed Bin Talal Alsaud, an entrepreneur and international investor, was born in 1955 on March 7 in Saudi Arabia. He is the second son of Prince Talal. In 1979, he completed Bachelor of Science degree in Business Administration from Menlo College and in 1985 he received Master's degree in Social Science from the Maxwell School of Citizenship and Public Affairs of Syracuse University.

He has also received an honorary PhD from the University of Exeter. His father was the brother of the king of Saudi Arabia, his parental grandfather Abdulaziz ibn Saud formed the kingdom of Saudi Arabia and maternal grandfather was the first Prime Minister of the Republic of Lebanon. He is widely known as a self-made billionaire who crossed the billion dollar mark at the age of 31.

He built up his large fortune by investing money in industries such as banking and finance, construction, media, hotels, technology and entertainment. From childhood, he has been intelligent with sharp mind and exceptional command over English, French and Arabic.

He possesses many aircrafts such as an Airbus 321, a Hawker Siddeley 125 and a Boeing 747 for private use and has the yacht Kingdom 5KR, with a helicopter on board.

By the end of 2012 he will have the world's largest passenger aircraft an Airbus A380.

Alsaud has 100 percent stake in Rotana Video & Audio Visual Company, 7 percent of Al Nahar and 25 percent of Al Diyar, 7 percent of News Corp (Fox News); about 6 percent of Citigroup, 90 percent ownership of Lebanese Broadcasting Center (LBCSAT), 95 percent stake in Kingdom Holding Company and two daily newspapers of Lebanon.

Philanthropic work:

He contributes to Centers of American Studies and Research in Middle Eastern universities and Centers of Islamic Studies in Western universities to improve the standard of education and eliminate the distance between Islamic and Western communities.

In 2001, after September 11 attack in New York, he contributed $10 million for the recovery. He donated $17 million to victims of 2005 Indian Ocean earthquake. He has contributed $20 million to Harvard University in 2009. He contributed 18.5 million British pounds to Palestinian families victimized by Israel violence in 2002.

According to Forbes Magazine 2010, he is the world's 19th richest man whose net worth is $19.4 billion. Time Magazine has given his nickname as the Arabian Warren Buffett.

Al-Waleed bin Talal Success Story

Quick Facts

One of Saudi Arabia's biggest visionaries and businessmen, Prince Al Waleed bin Talal is an inspiration to millions of businessmen out there who wish to sustain a family business and take it further beyond the realms of imagination. Born in Jeddah, he is the head of The Kingdom Holding Company and is one of the most influential people in the world, according to Time- a testament to his personality and business ethics.

He is mainly known as the Chief Executive Officer of the KHC and through his hard work and effort, the company had emerged as a leader in various sectors in the Saudi Arabian kingdom, including banking and finance, hotel management, mass media, entertainment, retail and agriculture to name a few. Apart from this, he is also the owner of some of the world's best known hotels and production companies, including the Four Seasons Hotel George V in Paris and the second-largest voting shareholder of 21st Century Fox.

Early Career

Initially, Al-Waleed was a troublesome child as he had not come to terms with his parents' separation. His father was the finance minister of Saudi Arabia in the early 60's. Prince moved to Lebanon with his mother after they separated. It was here that he would run away from home to sleep in the back of unlocked cars. His mother then decided to enrol him in a military school in Riyadh. He adopted a strict disciplinary code while he was there and continues to abide by them even today.

He received his Bachelor of Science degree from the Menlo University in California before obtaining his master's degree in Social Science from the Syracuse University. His story of riches began when he moved back to Saudi after his degree and was lucky to be caught up in the middle of the oil boom during 1974-1985, during which he got a large number of construction contracts which helped him amass a great fortune. He then turned the fortunes of the United Saudi Commercial Bank around by forming mergers. Bin Talal rose to prominence however, when he bailed out Citicorp during the early 90's with an investment of close to $550 million. Now, his shares are worth a billion dollars a testament to his smart investing and excellent market analysis.

He is also known to be a very friendly man and has made a lot of donations to charitable causes around the world. Such is his work in philanthropy that he has donated close to $50 million for charity."If I'm going to do something, I do it spectacularly or I don't do it at all." - Al-Waleed Bin Talal bin Abdulaziz al Saud.

Today, he remains one of the most respected businessmen, not only in Saudi Arabia, but all over the world. His economic reforms have helped transform his under-performing company to one of the best in the world.

ALIKO DANGOTE

Aliko Dangote, the First Nigeria's Billionaire was born on the 10th of April year 1957. He is the founder of Dangote Group. He is considered one of the richest men in Africa. He said "I assume I have to be rated by Forbes magazine prior to being called the richest man in Africa" ''But, you know, I'm very comfortable''.

"He ranked first in Nigeria in Forbes Magazine's 2008 list of the richest people in the world with a fortune estimated at 3.3 billion dollars. Aliko Dangote is the 'golden child' of Nigerian business circles. The Dangote consortium spans across numerous sectors of the Nigerian economy. The Dangote Group supplies commodities like cements, sugar salt, flour, rice, spaghetti, fabric etc at very competitive prices.

As a nonpartisan and detribalized businessperson, he is generous to different political parties, religious groups and cultural institutions. Apart from offering employment opportunities to elite graduates from different ethnic backgrounds, he reduces the level of crime by engaging youths who are school leavers in the area of transportation product packaging, security amidst others.

It may possibly not be a wild assumption to say that all Nigerian has heard of his name due to the impact of his business. His goods are practically in most homes across the country. People who may not use his products might have passed a few of his trailers by the way.

He's into exporting, importing, manufacturing, real-estate and philanthropy. All of these are combined together to form what is known as the Dangote Group. At the helm of its affairs as president and CEO is definitely an humble person called Aliko Dangote. The focus of his investments is food, clothing as well as shelter.

The Dangote Group imports 400,000 metric tonnes of sugar annually which makes up about 70 % of the total requirements of the nation and is a major supplier of the product to the manufacturers of Coca Cola, Pepsi Cola and Seven-Up in Nigeria.

It imports 200,000 metric tonnes of rice annually just as the company imports tonnes of cement and fertilizer and building materials. Dangote Group also imports fish and owns three big fishing trawlers chartered for fishing with a 5,000 MT capacity. The group exports cotton, cocoa, cashew nuts, sesame seed, ginger and gum Arabic to several countries globally.

His Beginning

Born in Kano, his grand father, the late Alhaji Sanusi Dantata provided him with a small capital to start his own business, as was the practice then. He thus started business in Kano in 1977 trading in commodities and also building supplies.

Alhaji Aliko Dangote moved to Lagos in June 1977 and persisted in trading cement and commodities. Encouraged by tremendous success and increase in business activities, he incorporated two companies in 1981. These as well as others that followed now make up the conglomerate known as The Dangote Group.

Dangote Group today is associated with diverse types of manufacturing with good revenues. Dangote textile and the Nigeria Textiles Mills Plc, which it acquired, produce over 120,000 meters of finished textiles daily. The Group has a ginnery in Kankawa, Katsina State with a capacity of 30,000 MT of seeded cotton annually.

The sugar refinery at Apapa port, Lagos is the largest in Africa and in size the third largest worldwide with an annual capacity of 700,000 tonnes of refined sugar annually. It also has another 100,000 tonne capacity sugar mill at Hadeja in Jigawa State.

Besides having significant investment in the National Salt Company of Nigeria at Ota, Ogun State, the Group has salt factories at Apapa as well as Calabar, a polypropylene bagging factory which produces essential bags for its products, over 600 trailers for effective distribution network and goods meant for export can also successfully be transported to the respective ports.

A vehicle leasing unit with over 100 fully air-conditioned commuter buses, is also part of the Dangote Group. It is also into real estate with luxury flats and high rise complexes in Ikoyi, Victoria Island, Abuja and Kano. Dangote Foundation is the philanthropic arm of the Group where yearly he spends millions for worthy causes such as contributions to educational and healthcare institutions, sinking of boreholes and giving of scholarships.

The Dangote Group has nationwide staff strength of 12,000 but on completion of on-going projects, it is expected to hit 22,000. Alhaji Aliko Dangote's business success may be influenced by various factors. He seems to be broad-minded. Unlike some people, his Personal Assistant is Yoruba while his Head of Corporate Affairs is a Christian from Delta State .

In this encounter, Dangote talks about his driving force in business, the factors that have kept him above his contemporaries in business, his $800 million cement factory at Obajana, Kogi State and the N14 million mega company, which he and some industrialists have set up. Perhaps above all, his patriotic stance is commendable: "If you give me today $5 billion, I will not invest any abroad, I will invest everything here in Nigeria. Let us put our heads together and work."

As a self-employed person, with minimum basic education, he proves that business success is usually through strength of mind, honesty and perseverance; and not necessarily by obtaining Harvard-Oxford certificates or First-Class academic qualification. His managerial skills surely are the envy of economic professors

Instead of stashing his funds in foreign accounts, a typical feature of fraudulent front and public office looters, Dangote invests wisely in the productive sector of the Nigerian economy. To deny that Dangote doesn't have monopoly over a few of the commodities in the Nigerian market is to deny the obvious.

AZIM PREMJI

Azim Hashim Premji, an Indian engineer, businessman and chairman of Wipro Limited, was born in 1945, July 24, in Mumbai, India, to a Gujarati Khoja Shia Ithna-Asheri Muslim family. He is the son of M.H. Premji who had established Western India Products that would manufacture hydrogenated vegetable fats and oil, hair care soaps, and ethnic ingredient based toiletries.

He completed his schooling from St. Mary's School, Mumbai and at the age of 21, attended Stanford University, California, to complete his studies in electrical engineering. However, he could not further his studies and had to return to take over the family business after the sudden death of his father in 1966.

After his joining in his father's company, Western India Products (he later renamed it Wipro Technologies and Wipro Corporation) and started expanding it to developing light bulbs with general electric, baby care products and shampoos, powders and other consumer products. In 1975, it began manufacturing hydraulic cylinders and truck tippers. In 1980 the company entered into IT sector and under a special license from Sentinel, it started developing computer hardware, software and related items. Wipro has won PCMM Level 5 and SEI CMM level 5 certification and has remained among the world's top 100 IT companies.

It is also one of the world's largest BPO companies and employs over 22,000 employees.

Awards and Recognition:

Business Week named him as one of the Greatest Entrepreneurs for making Wipro one of the world's fastest developing companies.

In 2000, he received an honorary doctorate from the Manipal Academy of Higher Education.

In 2004, Time Magazine kept him among its 100 most influential people in the world.

In 2005, he was honored with Padma Bhushan.

In 2008, on 58th Convocation Ceremony of the University, Aligarh Muslim University honored himwith a Doctor of Letters (D.Litt.).

In 2009, Wesleyan University in Middletown awarded him with an honorary doctorate for his philanthropic work.

Philanthropic Work:

Azim Premji has chiefly contributed to establish Azim Premji Foundation and has donated $2 billion worth of shares.

According to Azim Premji Foundation, it "Aims at making a tangible impact on identified social issues by working in active partnership with the Government and other related sectors of society" and Programmers offered are mainly for "creating effective and scalable models that significantly improve the quality of learning in the school and ensure satisfactory ownership by the community in the management of the school". This foundation "dedicates itself to the cause of Universalization of Elementary Education in India". It has successfully improved the quality of general education, mainly in rural schools.

Forbes magazine named him the Bill Gates of India for his Charity work. In 2011, he was the fifth richest man in India. According to Forbes Magazine 2011, he is the world's 36th richest person with $13 billion fortune.

ROBERT KUOK

Robert Kuok Hock Nien, a Malaysian businessman of Chinese origin, was born in Johor Bahru, Johor, on October 6 1923. He was the son of a well-off commodities trader who migrated to Malaysia in the beginning of the 20th century in pursuit of better prospects. Today, Kuok owns multiple enterprises across Malaysia and has investments across the countries like Australia, Fiji, Singapore, Philippines, Mainland, Thailand, Indonesia and China including 10 bottling companies of Coca Cola.

He also owns the Beijing World Trade Centre. Kuok's diverse business interests include the fields of sugar refineries, sugarcane plantation, oil, mining, finance, trading, properties, freight, and publishing. He owns Transmile Group, for transporting freight between India and China by air, and stakes in Malaysia International Shipping Corporation.

Robert Kuok completed school education from Raffles Institution in Singapore. After completing his graduation, he started his career as a merchant of Sugar, wheat flour and rice. However, Kuok claims that the first job he took up was working as an office boy. Between 1942 and 1945 he served in Japanese industrial conglomerate Mitsubishi, a grain department; and in 1949, he founded the Kuok Brothers Sdn Bhd to invest in sugar refineries. In 1957

Malaysia became independent and he started expanding his business across the country. In 1961, he began buying cheap sugar from India and selling it to Malaysia. Soon, he controlled 80% of sugar market of the country with 1.5 million tones productions. He achieved the title of 'The Sugar King of Asia'.

In 1971, Robert Kuok established the first Shangri-La Hotel in Singapore. He founded his second hotel the Kowloon Shangri-La at the Tsim Sha Tsui East waterfront in 1977. In the year 1993, his company the Kerry Group purchased a 34.9% stake in the South China Morning Post from Rupert Murdoch's News Corporation and the same year on April 1, 1993, he officially retired from the company and started living in Hong Kong. He has also been chosen as one of the representatives of the Hong Kong sovereignty.

Kuok Group has sold two of its sugar industries in Malaysia for $365 million. According to Forbes Magazine 2011, he is the world's 61st richest person with $12.5 billion fortune.

Profile

Among the most successful Asian, self-made industrialists who rule the business-world, Robert Kuok, the Malaysian billionaire, is a living legend. No one would perhaps have had as many businesses as him, all of them so huge. Robert Kuok, 91, had tried his hand in sugar-cane, oil, mining, flour, hotels, publishing and animal feed businesses, striking a huge success in whatever he touched. Kuok's story is one of those inspiring rags-to-riches saga. His uphill climb started as an office-boy, after which he became the clerk of a rice trading department in Singapore.

Robert Kuok however, was a quick learner. Three years in the rice trading department helped him learn the trading business. He later began back the same in his home town of Johor along with his brothers and a cousin. Shortly after that, he founded the Malayan sugar manufacturing co, which quickly gained popularity. It went on to become a monopoly in sugar production space of Malaysia producing 80% of Malaysia's sugar and 10% of world's sugar.

That's precisely how Kuok got his nick name, 'The Sugar King of Asia'. Establishing monopoly was not easy. "Have you ever seen Michael Jordan play when he's on a rhythm run? It was exactly like that" Kuok says modestly. Naturally, this ambitious and immensely clever businessman did not just stop at that. He started a chain of hotels, the famous 'Shangri-la' which is now spread out through the world and is all set to open its 71st hotel.

Robert Kuok's Success Story

The 91 year old now has a lot of investments in huge businesses in nearly all of the Asian countries, Indonesia, Australia, Malaysia, Singapore, Philippines, Indonesia and lot of other non-Asian countries. With so many businesses in so many countries, this incredible business man believes that he is the "little string that ties the rings together". Experts would often say that his speed and cleverness led to that near-impossible success.

Also, the man, they say, was never afraid to collaborate with the rest of the world unlike the Eastern businessmen of the early 20th century and that was one more thing that led to him being one of the most successful businessmen of the East. As per the Forbes list, Robert Kuok was declared the Richest Man of Malaysia and the Second Richest in South East Asia. In the Forbes' list of the richest men of 2013, he was ranked at 76th place. Kuok, who is now retired, will always be revered as one of the foremost eastern businessmen who gave birth to multinational business ventures for Malaysia and the world. His talent in business is unparalleled and his story continues to awe and inspire a lot of businessmen throughout the globe.

FRED DELUCA

Subway is the fastest growing fast food chain in the world. Founded in Connecticut, America, in 1965, as of 2010, they had over 1000 stores than McDonald's in the world. In 2013, Subway has more than 40,700 restaurants all over the world. The founder of 'Subway' Fred DeLuca started off in the food industry by opening a sandwich shop at the age of 17 in order to raise funds for paying his college fees. Young Fred did not want to be a businessman but a medical doctor. He got a loan of $1000 from a close friend who encouraged him to go ahead in setting up a restaurant. In 1965, he and his friend Peter Buck started their first venture together which they called 'Pete's Super Submarines'.

The long oblong shaped bun dish was a novelty and they hoped that it would click with the neighborhood crowd. They formed Doctors Associates Inc to oversee the running of their shops as a tongue in check reference to Fred's Medical aspirations and Peter Buck's Doctorate that they had originally tought of funding through this idea.

History and Early days

But by the end of the summer instead of making their first profits they had only $6 remaining with them. Instead of being disappointed and dropping out they went on to open another restaurant nearby. Again this was not able to reach the expectations that they had set for themselves. They defied logic and went on to open a third store this time renaming it as 'Subway'.

This time they were able to make profits of $7000 in its first full year of running. After experiencing their first success, Fred decided that he wanted to pursue his career in the food industry.

Milestones

He decided that by 1974 they would open 30 similar stores in their state. But 10 years passed and they could open only 16 stores in Connecticut. But again they found maintaining the quality of all the stores at the same level a difficult task. DeLuca realised that the franchise model was the best for any store looking for rapid expansion. So he persuaded his friend Brian Dixon to open the first Subway franchise in Walling ford, New Haven.

In that same year they were able to open another 14 restaurants using the franchise business model. Fred created the principles which all the 'Subway' restaurants needed to follow. High quality, fresh food and customer satisfaction were the pillars which the franchises needed to keep up. Success soon followed Subway as it was able to open its 100th store by 1978. The company made it compulsory that the bread that was used should be baked in the restaurant itself. This helped increase Subway's reputation and demand as the quality of the product increased. In 1984, they opened their first restaurant outside North America and that was in the island of Bahrain. In 1987, Subway had opened its 1000th store and in the year 1998 it opened its 10,000th store.

Now it started expanding itself to almost all the countries in the world including U.A.E., Norway, Pakistan, Hong Kong, Switzerland, etc. In 2000 it began a media campaign that would impact sales of Subway products everywhere in the world. In the campaign a 22 year old Jared Fogle claimed that he had lost 111 kilos eating only Subway sandwiches. This boosted Subway's fresh food ideology. As America was struggling with high obesity levels due to fast food eating trend, Subway became the best option to choose.

In 2002, Subway became the franchise with the highest number of outlets overtaking long time leader McDonald's. As of 2013 Subway has branches in 102 countries and yearly revenue of $9 billion. From being a part time business, Subway has become one of the most popular chain restaurants in the world. Their consumer oriented approach has made them one of the most successful companies of all time.

COLONEL SANDERS

Colonel Sanders' Background

Growing up in Indiana, household responsibilities were often left to him while his mother worked to support the family after his father's early death. This is how he developed his keen cooking skills as he helped his mother take care of the other children in his family. Several different jobs later, Sanders began his entrepreneurial career running a service station in Kentucky while serving his special chicken in a dining area within.

As business grew, he relocated to a restaurant close by in order to make his original recipe with its blend of eleven herbs and spices accessible to even more customers. He also added a motel to the business.

In 1935, at forty-five years old, Sanders was dubbed a Kentucky Colonel by the Governor, in recognition of his fabulous cooking skills. Subsequently, in 1940 Sanders created his well-known "Original Recipe."

Colonel Sanders' New Cooking Technique

Sanders originally prepared his chicken in an iron skillet but soon realized that was not efficient in a restaurant setting. In order to decrease the waiting time for his customers, Sanders modified his cooking procedure by making use of a pressure fryer.

Colonel Sanders' Entrepreneurial Drive

The Sanders Court & Café catered mainly to travelers on their way to Florida through the town of Corbin, Kentucky. However, in the early 1950's, a new interstate was in the works that would cause a great loss in business, forcing Sanders to retire and sell his restaurant. However, the government check was small and Sanders wasn't willing to just sit still and try to make due. He believed there was an opportunity to market his chicken to restaurant owners across the U.S.

In his travels, he was rejected on many occasions, laughed at about his attire of his starched white shirt and white pants. However, Sanders persevered, and after a little over 1,000 visits, he finally persuaded Pete Harman in South Salt Lake, Utah to partner with him. They launched the first "Kentucky Fried Chicken" site in 1952.

In the early 1960's there were over 600 franchised locations in the U.S. and Canada selling the delectable chicken. Subsequently, in 1964 Sanders sold the franchising operation for $2 million. The franchise has been sold three other times since then and continues to be a well-known successful business.

Sanders was born in 1890. When Sanders was 5 yrs old, he lost his father. His mother who was a housewife had to go out to work to earn for family and Sanders had to take care of his siblings.

He used to look after and cook for them. By the age of 7 his skills in cooking improved. At the age of 10, he began to work at local farmer. Soon, his mother remarried and Sanders had tumultuous relationship with his stepfather due to which he dropped out of 7th grade and left his home by himself.

At the age of 14, he took job for painting horse carriages and then moved to Indiana to work as farmhand for 2 yrs. At the age of 16 he falsified his date of birth and completed his service commitment as teamster in Cuba.

At age of 19 he met Josephine while working on rail road. Soon, he got married to her. They had three kids (son and two daughter). His son died at early age. Now, he found a job at Illinois central railroad but soon had to lost even this job due to brawl with his colleague and his wife left him and moved to her parents with kids.

He used to study Law by correspondence. After losing job he started to practice law but even his Legal career ended after a fight with his own client. He moved back to his mother and again went to work as labor for railway. Here he started to work as Life insurance agent but eventually fired.

At age of 30, he established a ferry boat company which was an instant success. After 3 yrs he sold all his shares of ferry boat for $22,000 and used this money to establish a company manufacturing lamps but even this venture failed. After this Sanders moved to Winchester, Kentucky to work as salesman but soon he lost his job also.

In 1930, Sanders was offered a rent free station to run by Shell oil company where he began to serve chicken dishes and other meals. Slowly his popularity grew and soon his service station became famous throughout Kentucky. It was called "Kentucky Fried Chicken of Harland Sanders." All customers noted the quality of its seasoning, which he prepared from 11 different spices. Life began to improve.

Harland Sanders bought a service station, motel and cafe at Corbin, a town in Kentucky. He left Claudia, as manager of the North Corbin restaurant and motel. He started to work as assistant cafeteria manager in Tennessee. In 1947 he divorced his first wife and in 1949 married Claudia.

For first time Sanders franchised "Kentucky Fried Chicken" in 1952. Restaurants sales lead to popularity of KFC and increase in income but life hit hard on him once again, due to some reason his sales dropped drastically and he was forced to sell all his property to pay his debt.

At age of 65 he was broke and was living off on Social Security Check of 105$. At this time he started to think about all and upon reflection he decided that he can sell his recipe to other restaurants. He wandered throughout U.S. with his spice recipe and pressure cooker visiting restaurants of America. Even this time it took long before he could find his first customer. After 4 years KFC was very successful and after a deal his net worth was estimated at $3.5 million. In 1980, at the age of 90 years, Harland Sanders died. In recent years he was traveling, playing golf and ran their own restaurant Claudia Sanders Dinner House with his wife.

WALT DISNEY

Few people embody the idea of a Renaissance man like Walt Disney. The entertainment tycoon was one of the most successful figures of the 20th century, building an empire that reached from its parks and resorts to home entertainment; from feature films and Academy Awards to philanthropic efforts around the world. While the Disney Corporation is likely to be forever associated with California, and Hollywood in particular, Walt Disney's story actually began in Illinois.

Born in the Chicago suburbs to parents that emigrated to America during the California Gold Rush period, Disney's childhood was filled with movement – his parents moved from farms to cities numerous times during his childhood. Disney's love of drawing and simple, charismatic artwork developed when he was a young boy. In his spare time, he would draw stylized versions of the farm animals near his home, drawing praise from his parents and neighbors. After being rejected from the Army at age sixteen during the First World War, Disney set about pursuing a career in animation – at the time an advanced form of art.

During an early job as an advertising artist, Disney discovered commercial animation. He quit his job and pursued animation as a full-time career, seeing fantastic potential in the newer cel-based forms of animation than in its predecessors. To call Disney's theory foresight would be a massive understatement – cel animation would eventually form the backbone of his company. From Chicago to Kansas; Kansas to Los Angeles, Disney eventually ended up opening his own animation company in Hollywood, California.

They invested in numerous cartoon characters and stories during their early years, including developments like Alice's Wonderland and the hit 1930s character – and now iconic symbol of Disney – Mickey Mouse. While Mickey was officially created in the late 1920s as 'Willie' – as seen in the iconic 'Steamboat Willie' cartoon, the iconic figure didn't reach its extreme levels of popularity until a few years later. It was this foresight and willingness to invest in characters without any idea of their potential that was so instrumental in Disney's success, and so iconic about his character. From Snow White to Pinocchio, Disney's company stormed through the 1930s and 40s with hit after hit, making it the most powerful animation studio in the world.

However, the studio was left with a single disappointment from this period, which would eventually go on to become one of the studio's most important films: the retelling of classic Austrian tale Bambi. Following World War II, Disney expanded his empire into theme parks and television, creating the empire that most are familiar with today. However, at the peak of the company's success in the mid 1960s, feeling fatigue from a polo injury that had caused him mild neck pain for years, Walt Disney sought the advice of his doctor regarding surgery.

The surgery's preparation exposed something alarming – Disney had a tumor in his lungs, which was quickly spreading throughout his body. Later in the month, on December 15th, 1966, Disney died at the St. Joseph's Hospital in Palm Springs. His death shook the world, but Disney's company remains a major force in media and entertainment today, over forty years after his sudden death.

The Walt Disney Company, founded by Walter Elias Disney and his brother Roy in 1923, is perhaps the world's most recognized brand. With more than $30 billion in annual sales, it's also the world's largest media company. Disney's numerous innovations include animated cartoons with synchronized sound tracks, the first full-length animated feature film, and theme parks such as Disneyland, Disney World, and Epcot Center.

AKIO MORITA

He was the man in charge of creating one of the most innovative companies of all time, Sony. However, it was not all smooth sailing, and he had his heeds of failure like many visionaries before and after him.

He initially began his entrepreneurial journey by creating a rice cooker that would actually burn the rice. This first so-called invention actually only sold under 100 units and the company folded immediately. This first major setback didn't stop him, in fact it fuelled motivation and gave him some big lessons on the business world and it's many challenges.

Many would give up with a flop like this, however, Morita kept his enthusiasm very alive and he kept trying, this time more calculated and creative. Eventually he would build the multi-billion dollar Sony empire...

The Sony Corporation was founded by Akio Morita and Masaru Ibuka in the year 1946 and registered as TTK (Tokyo Telecommunications Engineering Corporation). They started off by borrowing $500 to start developing consumer products. Their first product was a rice cooker which was a major failure and was unable to live up to its expectations. It grossed nearly $6500 in sales but was only able to bring in profits of $300.

But they were not discouraged by their failed attempt and went on to invest more capital for research. They were focussed on developing consumer products that would be useful to the population in Japan.

In 1950 their first product that was released was the tape recorder which was a replica of an American model that Ibuka had seen at the Japanese Broadcasting Corporation. There was not much demand for the product until they marketed the product by giving away copies of the Japanese translation of 'Nine Hundred and Ninety-Nine Uses of the Tape Recorder'.

When people released that this was such a useful product the local people ahead to buy the product and this made the product a huge success. With large orders coming from corporate companies and media houses, the company had to move to a larger facility to increase their production. In 1952 they added the transistor into their device and called the TTK radio as 'Sony'.

They used the term Sony because it came from 'Sonus' which is the Latin word for sound. In 1995 the company began mass-production of these Sony radios. This product became a rage among the common folk and beat the sales of its previous product by 1000%. As the name Sony began to become familiar with the people, the founders decided to name the company as 'Sony Corporation' in January 1958. The next decade they dominated the market with their videotape technology. In 1971, they released the first VCR

(Video Cassette Recorder) which received an Emmy award for engineering brilliance.

They developed a compact cassette tape player that was paired with light weight headphones. This device was called the 'Walkman' and could be used to listen to music while walking. This device became such a big hit that people used the term Walkman to describe cassette players that were produced by their competitors as well. In 1982 after lots of revenue being spent on research and development, Sony created the ground breaking product called the CD (Compact Disk) Player.

In 1985 they introduced the Video camera which soon became the best seller in many markets including North America, Europe and Japan. In 1992, Sony's total revenue stood at $1.3 billion.

In 1984 Sony released its mega-successful video game PlayStation for the first time. Sony ventured into producing television screens, smart phones, laptops and met with equal successful in all its new ventures. Sony's quality has been the backbone behind the immense trust that people have on their products.

As of 2013, they have more than $70 billion in yearly revenue. Sony has been a company that always anticipates the demands of the consumer and create revolutionary products to satisfy the customer. Sony has been a company whose success cannot be replicated in the decades to come.

ANDREW CARNEGIE

Andrew Carnegie, a Scottish-American industrialist and the greatest philanthropist in his epoch, is known to be the most influential person whose greatest contribution in expanding the American steel industry in 19th century makes him immortal. He donated his most of the fortune to establishing schools, libraries, and universities across the United States and Europe. He was a self-made man for his economic, cultural as well as intellectual developments. He is often considered to be the second richest man in history after John D. Rockefeller.

From his young age he would love to listen about famous Scottish heroes such as Rob Roy, William Wallace, and others from his uncle. The inspirational stories, in his words, worked as driving force for his life and inspired him to keep looking for better opportunities.

In 1848, his family immigrated to the United States, where he started working in a bobbin factory as an ordinary factory worker. Young Andrew worked almost all the day 6 days a week as a bobbin boy to make only $1.20 a week. His father was a weaver, and his mother bound shoes to make a living. He and his parents shared half of a considerably big, ground floor apartment with another poor family.

After some time, he became a messenger boy in the Pittsburgh Office of the Ohio Telegraph Company, at $2.50 per week. Within one year he was promoted as an operator for his determination, alertness and hardworking nature. In 1853, he took up a job at Pennsylvania Railroad as a secretary/telegraph operator at a salary of $4.00 per week. In less than three years, Carnegie was promoted to the post of superintendent. While working for the railroad, Carnegie got the opportunity to understand the infrastructure market and started making investments.

He could envision the greatest prospects in oil, steel and construction industries and made many wise choices that gave him substantial returns on investments. In 1864, he invested $40,000 at Story Farm in Pennsylvania and within one year his humble investment made him a millionaire. Finding the potential in steel, he invested in iron and subsidiaries. In 1865, after the end of the Civil War, he solely concentrated on the steel industry. Later, he merged Hi steel company with Federal Steel Company and several others and established the U.S. Steel.

In 2007, according to List of wealthiest historical figures, based on information from Forbes, his net worth was approximately amounted to $298 billion dollars.

HENRY FORD

Some businessmen creative innovative products. Others create massive fortunes. Very few create an entire system of production, an entire industry, and one of the world's biggest companies, all within the same time period. Henry Ford, one of the world's most important industrialists, is one of the few that have done such a thing, and his story remains one of the world's most inspiring and interesting.

ChildhoodBorn in 1863 in a small township that's now part of Detroit, Michigan, Henry Ford's early life was spent on a small rural farm. With a farmer for a father and a housewife for a mother, Ford's earliest years were spent surrounded by machinery. Impressed by farm equipment but uninterested in farm work as a career, he began training as a machinist in his late teens at a business in Detroit. Ford was known as a talented repairman, having assembled and repaired watches during his early childhood years.

His talents were soon put to the test as an engineer at the Edison Company, one of the city's pioneering mechanical corporations. He invested heavily in the company's projects, and in his own too, eventually creating the Ford Quadricycle, an invention that would contribute heavily to his later engineering feats designing motorcars.

After a series of investments with the Dodge brothers – a family that would later go on to create its own automobiles – Ford created a racing car. With almost one-hundred horsepower, it was one of the fastest vehicles of its generation, turning heads as well as dominating on the track. Seeing the potential of automobiles, Ford set out to create an inexpensive car for the American 'Everyman'.

Career

Seeing that the consumer-focused automobiles of his day were cumbersome and difficult to drive, Ford set out to create a car that anyone, given a few minutes of explanation, could control.

One of his first creations, and one of his greatest successes, was the Model T. Inexpensive yet high quality, it was an immediate hit with the middle class of America, and sold in immense quantities. To meet such high demand, and to stick with the model's low price point, Ford set out to create an innovative system of production. His production line system was an incredible development in its day, allowing Ford's workers to produce cars much more quickly than before.

His company made more cars than all others combined, all the while paying its workers higher wages than competitors. Ford has, as any automotive enthusiast will know, gone on to become one of the world's biggest and most successful car manufacturers. Many of the innovations that Henry Ford developed are normal within the engineering world today, including the semi-automated production line and higher-than-normal wages for engineers. His contributions to engineering are immense and widely celebrated. "If everyone is moving forward together, then success takes care of itself." - Henry Ford

Despite occasional criticisms due to his anti-Semitism and controversial 'social monitoring' tests for employees, Ford remains an icon of the industrial era and one of the business world's most valuable figures. A hard-working, intelligent, and street smart visionary, his long-lasting success proves that a great vision can result in hundreds of years of results.

DONALD TRUMP

Donald John Trump is the President-elect of the United States of America and will assume office as the 45th President of the country on January 20th, 2016. He'll be the oldest to do so, at the age of 70. He's a billionaire who's built several high-profile hotels, towers, casinos, etc,worldwide. He is also a reality TV star, and an heir, who now is President of The Trump Organization.

Childhood

Donald Trump was born on June 14, 1946. He is second youngest of the five children of his parents.

He was born to Mary and Fred Trump. He attended the Kew-Forest School in Jamaica Estates where he stayed in Trump family's two-story home Tudor Revival. Trump was known to be pretty rough as a child, not shying from tough drills.

Education

Trump did his schooling from the Kew-Forest School till he was 13. He then moved on to the New York Military Academy (NYMA). It was there in Cornwall, New York, where he finished his eighth grade and also high school. He performed his marching drills admirably and had earned the rank of captain during his senior years. He was a rough and daring child.

He studied at Fordham University in the Bronx for a period of two years. He was later shifted to the Wharton School at the University of Pennsylvania. He earned himself a Bachelor's Degree in Economics in the year 1968 from the Wharton School.

Early Life

From his political aspirations to his budding media empire, few business people are as enigmatic as the iconic Donald Trump. Known for his brash, ultra-confident demeanor, his business and lack of tolerance for imperfections, and, well, his hair, he's one of the United States' most controversial and public entrepreneurs, drawing attention no matter what he's involved in. However, Trump hasn't always been a massive success story.

Born on June 14th, 1946 to Fred and Mary Anne MacLeod in New York City, Trump has been associated with the city ever since. In the second half of the 20th century, his father transformed his small apartment rental business into one of the city's biggest low-income apartment empires, at one point owning over 27,000 rental units. This passion for real estate was passed over to his son, who quickly went into business with his father after finishing college.

Trump claims that he'd briefly flirted with the idea of a film career, preferring to focus on his creative side instead of commercial success. However, when he saw the suceessful business ideas gives potential in real estate, he quickly contacted his father and they started working together.

Career

Unlike many other entrepreneurs, Trump's career started out as an immediate success. After a brief sting working directly under his father, he was assigned new projects in Ohio to manage. During a tense time in New York City's economic history – the early 1970s – Trump started developing high-end office buildings and rentable spaces in Manhattan, considered a foolish idea at the time. Surprisingly, the scheme paid off, and Trump became an immediate success in the city.

Many of his buildings attracted both commercial clients and a great deal of praise from designers and the culture elite of the city. Trump had hit it big, and it seemed like his success would last forever."Sometimes by losing a battle you find a new way to win the war"-Donald John Trump. Throughout the 1980s, Trump expanded his empire further. He built casinos, created resorts in cities like Atlantic City and Las Vegas, and expanded his New York real estate holdings. He diversified to other markets, spreading his successful business ideas wide to protect against small failures. But it wasn't failure on a small scale that brought

Trump down, it was a massive failure in the country's economy.

Donald In the late 1980s, the country's economy stalled, bringing Trump's businesses, which were built on the basis of generating revenue from office rentals and luxuries, to a standstill. The developer hit a wall, and had to respond. He cut interest payments on his loans, sold off parts of his business, and very narrowly avoided having to file for personal bankruptcy.

Family

Donald Trump's family

Donald Trump, presently married to his third wife Melania Trump, has five children and eight grandchildren. From his first wife, Czech Model Ivana, he had Donald Jr, Ivanka, and Eric.

Trump was elected the 45th president of the United States. This was after his campaign got written off by the nation's political class. He defeated Hillary Clinton, the first female presidential nominee of a major party and a former first lady, senator from New York and secretary of state.

Net worth

Donald Trump's net worth

The present net worth of President-elect of the United States of America – Donald J Trump is US$3.7 billion, as of October 2016. He has earned his wealth through various businesses he has owned, his stints with reality television, and much of it has been bestowed upon him as a legacy of the Trump family.

Trump's businesses are far from their dark days of the late 1980s, they're no longer the gigantic empire that they once were. Trump's net worth is estimated at three-quarters of a billion dollars, a fairly impressive sum even with parts of his business less than ideal. The instant success kid may not be the biggest player in town anymore, but he remains a very successful man indeed.

SAM WALTON

Whenever we think of supermarkets, the first name that comes to our mind is Wal-Mart. Today the name is synonymous with retail shopping. A great mind often drives a successful business and one such person is Sam Walton. He started the first Wal-Mart in 1962 when he was 44 years old. The following years, discount chain stores expanded worldwide following his ideology.

Early Years

Born on March 29, 1918 in Kingfisher Oklahoma, Sam Walton grew up to be an over achiever. He was the first son of Thomas Walton and Nancy Lee. His parents played a large role in his success and Sam idolized his father to a great extent. During his school years he displayed tremendous amount of energy and enthusiasm towards studies. Everyone who knew Sam called him the most versatile boy.

Sam Walton as a college student

Walton studied with perseverance until he graduated from University of Missouri with a master's degree in Economics.

Even at a young age he showed keen interest in economics and business management. He soon proved to the world that large discount stores can thrive in business even in small rural areas.

Career

Sam Walton was first introduced to the retail market when he took up a job with J.C.Penney. At that time J.C.Penney was just beginning to step into the retail business.

That is when Sam Walton had a brain wave of starting his own retail chain. He borrowed USD$25,000 from his father-in-law and set up the first store in Newport, Arkansas. He did not stop there and continued opening stores in various other cities and towns. In a span of 2 decades, he was managing more than 15 retail stores across the United States. Sam Walton was a very hard working person.

He used to wake up at 4:30 AM to start working. The very kind of dedication led Wal-Mart towards quick success. In 1976, Wal-Mart went public with a net worth of $176 Million. By 1990, the stocks of Wal-Mart reached an all time high of $45 Million. In 1991, the company was richer than Sears and Roebuck and Company and came to be known as the world's largest retailer.

Personal Life

Even during the recession in 1991 and in times of economic turmoil, Wal-Mart sales increased by 40%. Sam was mainly responsible for wiping out local stores in communities of the United States. Walton, who was also a very generous and kind hearted person, compensated those individuals with jobs and donations through local charities. Despite his humungous success, Walton was a very humble man.

He drove a modest 1985 Ford Pickup truck. He was a true retailer by heart. He and his wife, Helen, lived in a small house built by then in Bentonville, Arkansas. He had 4 children - S. Robson, John, Alice and James.

Sam Walton Family to Death

After creating a retail empire in the United States, Sam Walton died on April 5, 1992. He left the ownership of the management to his wife and children. His legacy continues even after years of his death and he was also named among the top 100 most influential people by Fortune.

Every businessman tries to take a leaf out his life to make their own business as successful.

RAY KROC

Did you know that over 65 million people eat at McDonald's every day? Did you know that the McDonald's company serves over 100 million burgers every single day? Did you know that one of the world's largest restaurant chains grew from a small family restaurant in a California town?

McDonald's may be the world's most well known restaurant today, but it wasn't always a huge global success. Founded by Richard and Maurice McDonald in the early 1940s, McDonald's pioneered the 'Speedy Service System' – a simple method of preparing hamburgers that used production line efficiency in a restaurant.

The service and the restaurant, which served up simple hamburgers and family meals in a small California town, proved to be a hit. Tired of waiting for hours for their food in other nearby restaurants, visitors flocked to the brothers' restaurant for tasty, affordable food that arrived at their tables in mere minutes. Despite its success, however, it took McDonald's a surprisingly long time to become one of the world's top restaurant brands.

The company only filed for a trademark in 1961, describing itself as a 'drive through restaurant' and introducing its mascot – Ronald McDonald – in the same year.

McDonald's CEO Steve Easterbrook. Meanwhile, Ray Kroc, a Chicago-born businessman, was helping the brothers size up their business opportunities in Southern California. The company expanded to nine restaurants in the late 1950s and quickly became a leading franchise, with Ray Kroc turning the small company into a corporation and quickly buying up the equity. Over the next fifty years, McDonald's expanded from a small operation of around ten restaurants into the international juggernaut that it is today.

The restaurant initially expanded throughout the United States, saturating the market for fast food that had been invented by White Castle several years earlier, before it expanded overseas. Today, McDonald's maintains over 34,000 restaurants around the world, serving up everything from Breakfast McMuffins to unique dishes like the McShrimp.

One of the world's truly global corporations, McDonald's restaurants can be found in countries as far abroad as Indonesia and Egypt, where the company has a special halal menu.

McDonald's food story

This rapid expansion has earned the company both praise from business analysts and scorn from cultural preservationists, who claim that McDonald's has pushed its way into countries that didn't want it.

The company's ethics aside, its success as a global franchise is undeniable, and it is one of the 20th century's biggest successes.

McDonald's legacy

Over the years, McDonald's has pioneered several features of the fast food industry that modern customers take for granted.

From the introduction of a special morning breakfast menu in the 1970s to its incredible innovation in food preparation, there's a lot to thank McDonald's for. Whether you're a health guru or a loyal McDonald's fan, the company's expansion from a single California restaurant into one of the world's largest restaurant chains is undeniably one of America's greatest successes. From corporate culture to ultra efficient food preparation, McDonald's is a great example of an innovative success.

HOWARD SCHULTZ

To dream by night is to escape your life. To dream by day is to make it happen. Howard Schultz was born on July 19 1953 in Brooklyn, New York. He did his education in bachelors from Northern Michigan University. He became retail and marketing operations director in 1982. He purchased Starbucks in 1987 and also became the CEO of the chain in the later years.

Early Career

Howard Schultz was also the former owner of the Seattle Supersonics before becoming the CEO of Starbucks.

He was ranked as the 354th Richest Man in the US by Forbes in the year 2012. After graduating from the college he also worked as a sales person for Xerox Corporation. He always remembers the first time he went to the original Starbucks in the year 1981. At that time, the Starbucks did not exist beyond Seattle.

After a year, he joined Starbucks as the director of the sales and marketing operations for the coffee company. At that time, the company only sold coffee beans. In a span of a year only, he made Starbucks as the mission of the rest of his life. Then he got an idea that Starbucks should not only sell coffee beans, but also coffee drinks. This idea came while travelling through Milan, Italy. He did not share his idea with the company owners, but when they came to know about the idea, they were not at all convinced and refused to join him.

But after the success of the coffee drinks in the company, the owners of the company got frustrated. Schultz left the company and started his own chain of coffee bars, called Starbucks. He purchased the company with the help of the investors. He became the CEO of the company and the company got much success as expected. Starbucks is one of the biggest coffee bars to sell large number of coffee drinks in a number of places around the globe. By 2012, there were around 17,600 stores all over the world in around 35 countries.

The company opens a new store every day and has always attracted a number of customers towards it. In 2013, Schultz came in news for supporting the legalization of gay marriage. He got a great applause on this from the people. After losing the company's shares on supporting the gay marriage, he was not at all afraid of anything.

Made in the USA
Middletown, DE
30 August 2018